Save Your Heart with Susan

To Cathy—
A terrific and my
dietitian and my
new "agent." Thanks
for all your hard work.
Susan Nicholson

Save Your Heart with Susan

Six Easy Steps
to Cooking Delicious Healthy Meals
in a Microwave

Susan Nicholson,
R.D./L.D.

with Cynthia Jubera

WILLIAM MORROW AND COMPANY, INC.
NEW YORK

The information in this book is not intended for self-treatment. Consult your physician before using this or any other diet, to make sure it is appropriate for you.

The information in this book reflects the author's experiences and opinions and is not intended to replace medical advice. Any questions about your health should be directed to your physician.

Library of Congress Cataloging-in-Publication Data

Nicholson, Susan.
    Save your heart with Susan / Susan Nicholson with Cynthia Jubera.
      p. cm.
    Includes index.
    ISBN 0-688-09016-8
    1. Coronary heart disease—Diet therapy—Recipes. 2. Coronary heart disease—Prevention. 3. Microwave cookery. I. Jubera, Cynthia. II. Title.
    RC685.C6N53   1991
    641.5'6311–dc20   90-6502
                  CIP

Printed in the United States of America

First Edition

1 2 3 4 5 6 7 8 9 10

BOOK DESIGN BY MANUELA PAUL

To My Two Best Friends:

Judy Pattee,

who remembers everything good (and bad)
I ever said or did and still loves me,

and

Kay Maniha,

who taught me more than she could ever imagine,

and

to the children I wish were mine:

Jennifer and Josephine Raney,
Erica Abood and Erin Keenan,
and the twins
Eleanor and Amy Pattee,
and
Mark Maniha

Acknowledgments
❧❧❧

❧ To the special people who brought *Save Your Heart with Susan* to print (some directly and some not so directly):

First and foremost, my husband, Tex, participated all along the way during the writing of this book. In November 1988, he chained me to a chair in a cabin up in the North Georgia mountains, and made me write seven chapter headings (about forty-five words) that became *Save Your Heart with Susan*. He put up with my total involvement in the project and never complained. Well, almost never.

He tasted every recipe, good and not so good, and gave his objective, and always tactful, opinion. He liked every recipe that stayed in the book and had a large say in whether a recipe survived or not. He, much more than I, knew I could write a book, and believed in me all along the way.

My father, the world's best salesman—don't ever ride through my hometown of New Market, Virginia, even

thinking you need a new car—because he'll sell you one!
My father taught me to dance when I was about six years
old, and every time we're together, we still "cut a rug."

Fritz, my brother, and forever one of my heroes, is quiet,
and not at all like his sister. (How quiet is he? Very few
people know that his golfing honors include four *docu-
mented* "holes in one.") His wife, Loretta, contributed
many ideas and a good "ear."

I hope my mother has been taking all of this in. I can
see her in heaven, coming home from a day of teaching
the angels about the War Between the States and Stone-
wall Jackson's "Valley Campaign." When her students used
to ask, "Mrs. Orebaugh, did the North *ever* win a battle?,"
her reply was always, "Not while I'm teaching this course!"
A true and loyal Virginian, she had a great sense of humor
and tried to teach me everything she knew about cooking.

My mother-in-law, Becky, who will be known to you as
What's-her-name, who taught me even more about cooking and entertaining. She wanted to make sure her son ate
well. Her other son, the Gary's Grits guy, still laughs when
he thinks about Susie (that's me) cooking.

The daring ladies who ventured to California in the 1930s
with my mother: Marie Whitmore, Catherine Miller,
Samuella Crim, and Grace McCarthy. The friendships of
these women and their families enriched my childhood.

I owe a great deal to some former bosses who taught
me a lot over my working career: Fred Abood for his cool-
ness and calm; Mick Adamson for his Irish fierceness; and
Sal Mele for his New York "hyper." I learned from all of
you.

Registered dietitians I particularly admire and who gave
me their enthusiastic approval on a heart-healthy micro-
wave cookbook with a sense of humor: Martha Prater,
Flossie Hahn, Carol Frankmann, Rosemary Gaddy, Dee
Baxter, Molly Gee, Nancy Fong, Jana Kelly, Ardine
Kirchhofer, Avé Bransford, Olga Satterwhite, Jayne
Gilbert, Mona Boyd, Sandra Robbins, and Jeanne Delker.

Special dietitians contributed more than they realize. Missy Cody (Mildred) gave me many ideas and answered numerous questions. A professor at Georgia State, Dr. Cody supervised the nutritive analysis for all the recipes. Mary Joan Oexmann gave good advice. Mary Abbott Hess took time to explore ideas with me.

I would also like to thank: My former dietetic interns and students. You are what really makes "keeping up" fun. I am proud of all your successes. You are now *my* mentors.

The Friedman family in California who taught me all about microwaves.

Angela Mitchell, Gail Murphy, Helen MacDonald and Jackie Tulloh, who first taught me the wonders of micro-wave cooking.

Paul Libbe, the world's best microwave repair man, limerick writer, and recipe taster, who showed me how microwaves "work" and told me my cooking wasn't too bad.

Wendy Byrd and Susan Swett, who shared so many recipes.

For reviewing portions of the medical information in Chapter 2: Jerry Lutz, M.D., assistant professor of medi-cine (cardiology) at Emory University School of Medi-cine, and president of the American Heart Association, Georgia affiliate; Dallas Hall, M.D., director, division of hypertension, Emory University School of Medicine, and past president of the American Heart Association, Georgia affiliate.

For their advice and sharing of medical, nutritional, and technical information: Chris Lecos, public-affairs officer for the Food and Drug Administration, National Press Of-fice, Washington, D.C.; the many helpful people with the U.S. Department of Agriculture Nutrition Information Line, and other USDA departments; Basil M. Rifkind, M.D., F.R.C.P., chief of lipid metabolism—atherogenesis branch, National Heart, Lung and Blood Institute, National Institutes of Health, Bethesda, Maryland; Thomas High, M.D., Atlanta, Georgia; Van Hall, director of communications for the American Heart Association, Georgia affiliate; and cookbook author, Anne Lindsay.

People who answered my questions along the way: Bob Schiffman, Harry Rubbright, Bob LaGasse, Joan Toole, Thelma Pressman, Lorela Wilkins, Shirley Corriher, and Kay Goldstein.

So many other friends who allowed me to talk about them.

Elaine and Ingo Hentschel, who came for many "test" meals. Elaine made the Roast Pork with Honey Mustard Sauce one of her standards, and I was thrilled.

Donovan Fandre, the Microwave Master, who let me "tag along" with him to an Atlanta TV studio to see how a *real pro* does *live* TV cooking.

Those who propped me up when the TV cameras started rolling: Jill Becker, who "discovered" me and calls me her protégée, Tracy Green, Paula Sinkovitz, Marla Shavin, and the *Noonday* crew who were there to help me, and sample food. Wicke Chambers, who listened to me when I needed listening "to," and gave me encouragement for cooking on TV. Registered dietitians Carolyn O'Neil and Liz Weiss, who first took the message of *Save Your Heart with Susan* to an international television audience.

Another mentor-friend along the way is Susan Lawrence. She always answered every question and gave good advice. Someday she will find the kitchen in her own home!

And last but not least:

The man who *told* me to write a book, my agent, Bill Adler, and the woman who called me the first time and identified herself as "your editor." I appreciate her because she told me I did not have to become a "foodie," but just to have fun. She has her priorities in order, and because she does, so do I.

Contents

ชชช

(

Introduction

ⓏⓏⓏ

Dear Friends:

When I use that term, I really mean it. When some wonderful person first asked me to write this book, I gave a lot of thought to for whom I would write it. And I knew exactly who *you* would be.

You are part of a secret society of people who, like me, see cooking not as an art form but as something closer to torture—hanging from a cliff by my polished fingernails would be more fun than cooking a five-course meal. And forget dinner parties where the guests spend half the evening in the kitchen wielding rolling pins and copper bowls—you won't find that at my house! To me, and I think to you, too, cooking is a job to get through to get to the fun parts of life. And my hunch is that there are more of *us* than *them*.

You are also the people who have made my Save Your Heart with Susan cooking classes a standing-room-only success, who write me by the bushelful after a television show, and who came to my store in Atlanta to buy a microwave oven. I couldn't wait to tell you, and people just like you all over the country, what I've learned that will make your life simpler and healthier, just by using your microwave oven.

Then my "foodie" friends got hold of me.

I started listening to people who know a lot about food and take cooking seriously. My friends did their absolute best to turn me into a foodie too. (Foodies are people who will take a simple three-step, five-minute recipe and turn it into a twenty-step one that takes all day to prepare, just for the fun of it. This may be all they do for fun, since they don't have time for anything else.) These folks just love to ramble around a kitchen, as if they have all the time in the world, and rhapsodize about cooking. Suddenly, my days began and ended with cooking. I fell headlong into a crash course in gourmet cooking. I began using weird new ingredients and discussing the finer points of cooking techniques that I couldn't have been bothered with before. In general, I tried to be a foodie. But it just didn't work. I get no thrill from the ritual of cooking. I also get no thrill from cleaning up the mess. Instead, I get a thrill from eating.

Finally, a faraway friend put an end to the silliness. "For heaven's sake, Susan," she said. "Simply tell people about the way *you* cook, and how it can save their hearts."

So the book you are getting is not from a foodie. It's from someone, probably just like you, with the same problems of rushing home at six o'clock to a horde of hungry mouths screaming, "Feed me, feed me." Its purpose is to make your life easier, and you and your loved ones healthier.

The microwave cooks delicious food that is as healthy as food cooked any other way. It brings out natural flavors in foods, from broccoli to bluefish, and accentuates many spices (for more information on flavor, see page 290). Food cooked in the microwave is healthier because the microwave draws fat from the food, and many dishes can be cooked completely without fat, the culprit that we all know may increase the risk of heart disease. So I don't want to hear any of this "I'm-only-going-to-reheat" business. Remember your heart? We're trying to save it. Your microwave will become your best friend in the kitchen.

In *Save Your Heart with Susan,* you will find good advice on how to buy a microwave and the cookware you really need. Just enough heart-healthy lingo to keep you on track. You will find familiar recipes, ones that I guarantee are easy and taste good. Some are family meals—simple and quick—for the frantic days we all have. Other recipes, all pulled together into complete meals, you could serve to the most discerning guests.

I have tested these recipes countless times to make sure they worked the way I say they do. And to prove how easy the recipes are, I have prepared many of them on TV in five minutes or less. Just as I've taught thousands of others who have attended my Save Your Heart with Susan cooking classes and watched my television programs, I can teach you!

I also want you to have *fun* along the way. Cooking isn't a contest—so what if you turn a piece of bread into a rock? I have.

When you finish reading this book, I hope you will all burn a path to the kitchen, recipes in hand. With all the time you are going to have left, you can take a walk, or read a book, or, most of all, enjoy your family more.

And because you will be healthier, you just might live longer.

CHAPTER 1

How Save Your Heart with Susan Began

৫৫৫

A Little History

৫ "Susie, you'd better come home," said the voice on the other end of the telephone. It was my father. It was late at night, long past the time my father usually goes to bed. I braced myself. "Fritz has had a heart attack."

We're never ready when that phone call comes, and I certainly wasn't. Fritz was my only brother, and it seems, at age forty-seven, he had just had open-heart surgery and two massive heart attacks. There was no time to brood; I boarded a train to Virginia and rode all night. I had plenty of time to think about all the things we do wrong in our lives, what's important and what's not. And I thought a lot about my brother.

Five years younger than Fritz, as a kid I copied anything he did with a passion. He hated red; I hated red. He hated onions; I hated onions. He roller skated fast; I fell down and skinned my knees trying to keep up.

I threw away my cigarettes that night. Fritz smoked too.

And I promised myself to help my brother recover, any way possible. And the best way would be to learn how to eat to have a healthy heart.

You see, I'm a registered dietitian. Some dietitians work in hospitals, planning the menus for sick people. (In fact, I did that early in my career.) A few are righteous souls who never eat anything "bad." Not me—I loved my cheeseburgers and chips as much as the next person. But I knew how I was supposed to eat.

Fritz's heart attack came before the birth of my Save Your Heart with Susan classes. And it was the reason why they started.

The Hospital

I can still remember the words the nurse said to me that morning when I arrived at the hospital in Charlottesville after a twelve-hour train ride. "Mrs. Nicholson, the doctor would like to talk to you." My mouth went dry. I wanted to scream, *"What do you mean! Is he Dead or Alive?"* But instead I choked out gratefully, "How is he?"

The doctor reassured me and went on to explain charts and numbers and rehabilitation plans, most of which I did not hear. I just wanted to see my brother for myself.

Finally, I got my chance to "look" at him. The body I saw that Wednesday at 7:00 A.M. was *not* my brother. My brother always had a big grin on his face, and he certainly wasn't *that* color. I was almost afraid to touch him. When I finally did, I was relieved his skin was still warm.

Over three weeks' time, Fritz slowly recovered. By December 23, we checked him out of the hospital and headed for home.

We were the lucky ones; we went out the *front* door.

Home for Christmas

We were home for Christmas instead of at a funeral. No doubt that was the happiest Christmas our family ever had. The picture we took that day shows a lot of people with tired, thankful smiles.

Now what can he eat?

Talk about agony. Fritz may have been let out of prison, but he was definitely on parole.

Christmas dinner was easy enough. The mashed potatoes, of which he usually could eat a plateful, were made with skim milk. Turkey, now that was surely safe. Cranberries, no problem. Dressing, sorry, it was made with eggs and butter. We didn't mention the pumpkin pie. We spent most of the meal eyeing him, looking for signs of another attack.

In time Fritz got better; his "greenness" around the edges disappeared, and our changes began.

Is changing a lifetime of eating habits easy? Of course not. But for me, it took that one Significant Emotional Event (SEE) that psychologists talk about, my brother's attack, to make me change my habits. I changed. My husband changed. My brother and his wife changed. My mother tried to change. My father will never change.

It was after subtler eating, cooking, and flavoring changes, ones that could last through the long stretch.

I've managed to achieve the flavors I was after—even desserts, because I, too, love sweets.

Welcome to Retail

How I changed was a matter of pure chance.

I had recently purchased a small microwave shop.

Overnight, I went from never having owned or used a microwave to owning *five hundred* of them. Talk about baptism by fire—I learned about them, and fast! I was impressed with the microwave from the beginning—anything that got me out of the kitchen faster had my vote. I began to explore all the wonderful and delicious ways a microwave could make my life easier.

Now, after over five years of my teaching classes, my friends familiar with my attitudes toward cooking aren't laughing quite as hard or loudly as they did. That's because, with the microwave, I have become an enthusiastic cook.

I was warming to the idea that healthy food could taste great and look great too. And the more I taught, the better the recipes became, and the easier it was for me to develop simple, delicious ones. Since I am a registered dietitian, it was a short step to make them heart-healthy too.

Without my realizing it, Save Your Heart with Susan became more than a class I taught; it became my way of life.

CHAPTER 2

A Little Pep Talk Before We Cook

ભ્ર્ય્ર્ય

Heart Disease: Just the Facts, Madam

ଘ   Our lives are stressful, fast-paced, and chaotic.We don't eat right, exercise often, or relax enough. We dress out of the clothes dryer before work and eat dinner standing at the stove after work. This crazy lifestyle may leave us likely targets for heart disease.

Strokes, heart attacks, atherosclerosis, angina attacks, and high blood pressure are quietly killing millions of Americans, like a silent shadow settling over a city. And they don't happen overnight.

In spite of the good news that deaths by heart disease have declined 24 percent in the past twenty years, for Americans it is still the *leading* cause of death. In fact, victims of heart disease outnumber those of cancer, AIDS, accidents, and suicide *combined*. Heart disease is literally killing us every minute of every day.

Look at these figures from the American Heart Association:[1]

- Between the ages of 45 and 54, 72 percent men and 75 percent women have serum cholesterol over 200 mg/dl (or 5.17 millimoles) or more.
- 46 percent of Americans die of heart disease.
- 1,500,000 will have a heart attack this year. One third will die.
- One American dies from a heart attack every thirty-two seconds.
- More than one in four Americans suffer from some form of cardiovascular disease.
- 424,000 men between the ages of 45 and 64 and 374,000 women *over* 65 experience heart attacks.

I think living is just too much fun to put up with a half-life restricted by poor health. I hope you feel that way too. After I get you out of the kitchen with my quick-and-easy Save Your Heart with Susan recipes, you will feel better and have more time to pursue the life you love. With the people you love.

What you are about to discover is that cooking in the microwave oven is one of the healthiest ways you can cook to save your heart (and the rest of your body). With the microwave oven, you can cut back on calories and salt and never know the difference. You want moist, juicy meat without added fat? Long-simmered flavor without lots of salt and sugar? The secrets are all here, right in this book. Overall health is the goal, and cooking in the microwave makes that goal easier to achieve than ever before.

The benefits sound almost too good to be true—cooking in the microwave is easy, it saves a mess in the kitchen, the food tastes good, and *it's healthy*. Who could ask for more?

[1] Statistics from *1990 Heart and Stroke Facts* (Dallas: American Heart Association, 1989).

And no, you don't have to eat seeds and sprouts the rest of your life. That's why Save Your Heart with Susan menus always end with a wonderful dessert. I, too, have a sweet tooth. And because you discovered healthy microwave cooking *here,* with good shopping tips, good microwave-cooking instructions, and delicious recipes, you are on your way to the beginning of a new life!

What We Don't Know

From forty years and billions of dollars spent on research, authorities are confident that a relationship exists between diet and heart disease. As is usual, a controversy exists in scientific matters. Some studies found little relationship between lowering cholesterol levels and decreasing heart disease. Some studies have found little association between lowering blood pressure and lessening strokes. Some studies have found no relationship between stress and heart disease. *But most major studies found that fat affects heart disease.*

Of course, the matter isn't settled yet. Research continues. The biggest controversy revolves around which groups of people are most affected by cholesterol and which ones are less affected. As scientists get more information, they will continue to revamp their advice on how we should eat and live to lessen *our number-one killer—heart disease.*

Scientists, doctors, and dietitians reserve the right to change their minds. So don't begrudge them. It just means they are getting closer to something we all want—*the truth.*

Remember, quacks are the only ones who never change their tune.

What We Do Know

Just by changing the way we eat and cook, *we can lessen our chances of a heart attack.*

For maximum health and well-being, to reduce the risk of heart disease, some cancers, diabetes, and other so-called lifestyle diseases, most health authorities recommend:

- Eat a nutritionally adequate diet consisting of a variety of foods.
- Achieve and maintain a reasonable body weight.
- Reduce consumption of fat, especially saturated fat and cholesterol.
- Increase consumption of complex carbohydrates and fiber.
- Reduce intake of sodium.
- Consume alcohol in moderation, if at all. Children, adolescents, and pregnant women should abstain.

VARIETY IS THE SPICE OF . . .

Eat a variety of foods: We need more than forty different nutrients for optimal health. No single food supplies all of those nutrients, and most foods have more than one nutrient in them, whether it's protein, vitamins, minerals, fat, fiber, or carbohydrates. Our body needs all of them. The very best way to assure optimal health is to eat lots of different foods.

Don't skip breakfast and lunch. Instead, try to eat regularly—three or more meals a day (but don't eat more calories—just spread them equally throughout the day). So eat small meals regularly, and don't save up for one big meal a day. I don't *care* if you are going to Sonny's All You Can Eat Fish Fry tonight!

WEIGHT If you are overweight, you are at greater risk of developing diabetes, high blood pressure, and high cholesterol, all of which can lead to heart disease. For that reason alone, you should maintain a desirable weight.

To lose one pound a week, you have to cut about five hundred calories a day. Calories aren't the only answer, of course. The success of a weight-loss program also depends on physical activity and the amount of *fat* you consume. Many studies have found that people who cut calories but still eat a lot of fat have a harder time losing weight.

Tex and I both lost weight while I worked on this book. The recipes in *Save Your Heart with Susan* are low in fat and heart-healthy.

How Much Should You Weigh?

Use this Rule of Thumb formula to calculate your ideal body weight.[2]

For Women: Give yourself one hundred pounds for the first five feet, plus five pounds for each additional inch.

If you are 5′1″:   100 pounds
                    +   5 pounds for 1 inch
                        ─────

Your ideal weight is 105 pounds, plus or minus 10 percent for small, medium, or large frames.

For Men: Give yourself 106 pounds for the first five feet, plus six pounds for each additional inch.

If you are 5′10″:   106 pounds
                      + 60 pounds for 10 inches
                        ─────

Your ideal weight is 166 pounds, plus or minus 10 percent for small, medium, or large frames.

[2]Formula from the *Georgia Dietetic Association Diet Manual,* 3rd Edition, 1987.

AVOID TOO MUCH FAT, SATURATED FAT, AND CHOLESTEROL
Put Your Fat Intake on a "Budget"!

The secret to Save Your Heart with Susan recipes is cutting the fat and saving the flavor. The U.S. Dietary Guidelines recommend we get 30 percent of our calories from fat, and keep cholesterol below 300 mg each day. If you cut down on total fat, especially animal fat, you will also cut saturated fat and cholesterol. They go together.

All of the recipes in Save Your Heart with Susan list grams of fat. By looking at the recipes, you can easily add how many grams of fat you are eating each day. At nine calories a gram, fat is higher in calories than protein or carbohydrates, which both have four calories a gram. Look at how 30 percent of calories from fat breaks down:

If you eat:	Limit your fat to:	That's how many calories?
1,200 calories a day	40 grams fat	360
1,400 calories a day	47 grams fat	420
1,600 calories a day	53 grams fat	480
1,800 calories a day	60 grams fat	540
2,000 calories a day	67 grams fat	600
2,200 calories a day	73 grams fat	660

We know that three kinds of fats exist: *saturated, monounsaturated,* and *polyunsaturated.* All foods that contain fat contain a mixture of all three. When a food is said to be monounsaturated, that means it is *mostly* monounsaturated. Butter, for example, is considered saturated, but it is actually 51 percent saturated. Peanut oil, on the other hand, is considered a monounsaturated oil. In fact, peanut oil is 46 percent monounsaturated.

Health professionals tell us to divide our fat intake into roughly one-third saturated fat, one-third monounsaturated fat, and one-third polyunsaturated fat. To do that, simply limit animal fats and don't add additional fat to dishes. The fat you do use should be a monounsaturated fat (canola and olive oil) or polyunsaturated fat (corn or safflower oil) whenever possible. The beauty of cooking in your microwave is that it lets you cook most foods with *little or no fat.*

Saturated fats, like butter, are solid at room temperature. They raise the level of cholesterol in the blood. Saturated fats are usually found in animal products like meat, milk, and eggs. The exceptions are the tropical oils—coconut and palm oils. Coconut oil, for example, at 87 percent saturation, is the most saturated fat we know. Tropical oils like coconut oil are used widely in processed food to give a rich texture to baked goods and to make products last longer on the shelf. Because of pressure from health and consumer groups, many companies have changed their products, from cookies to microwave popcorn, and have replaced tropical oils with more unsaturated oils.

In a process called hydrogenation, fats often have hydrogen gas added to make them more shelf-stable at room temperature. Most of the polyunsaturated vegetable oils are partially hydrogenated. Vegetable *shortenings* are completely hydrogenated and remain solid at room temperature. Solid shortening is highly saturated.

Monounsaturated oils are liquid vegetable oils such as canola and olive oil. Research shows that monounsaturates are effective in lowering LDL blood-cholesterol levels while leaving the beneficial HDL cholesterol intact. Olive and canola oil are the two monounsaturated oils I have used in Save Your Heart with Susan recipes.

Polyunsaturated oils come from fish oils or are pressed from seeds such as corn, sunflower, and safflower, and are liquid at room temperature. (Often they will have been partially hydrogenated to prolong shelf life, as was mentioned earlier, or totally hydrogenated, as in shortening. Hydrogenation takes away the healthful benefits of vegetable oils.) Polyunsaturated oils also lower blood-cholesterol levels, but they lower both the LDL and HDL.

Although the recommendations are mixed, some studies recommend that the primarily polyunsaturated Omega-3 fatty acids found in fish, purslane (a salad green), canola oil, walnut oil, and some seeds may bestow extra protection against coronary heart disease. These fatty acids may lower triglycerides and cholesterol, and thin the blood to prevent blood clots. Early research shows that the Omega-3 fatty acids from fish are more easily used by the body than those from vegetable sources.

Don't waste your money or your health on fish-oil supplements (or any other supplements unless recommended by your personal physician). If you take Omega-3 fatty acids in a capsule, the fish oil becomes a drug, rather than part of a food in a balanced, healthy diet. The pills may not be effective because the amount of Omega-3 fatty acids in each pill varies. Also the amount of fat in an individual's diet affects the action of the Omega-3 fatty acids.

COMPLEX CARBOHYDRATES AND FIBER Health professionals recommend that 55–60 percent of our calories come from foods high in complex carbohydrates. That's over half of the calories we eat every day! Such a high percentage of our food translates to putting more rice, beans, and vegetables on your plate, and spreading around a small amount of meat.

Why? Because complex carbohydrate foods pack in the protein, vitamins, and minerals. And carbohydrates are still low in fat. Ounce for ounce, at four calories a gram, carbohydrates have less than half the calories of fat.

Complex carbohydrates give us a continuous supply of energy without boosting blood sugar too high or too fast. Bread, potatoes, rice, pasta, fruits, vegetables, and dried peas and beans are all good sources of complex carbohydrates. Many are the satisfying "comfort" foods we all crave—just the idea of a plate of mashed potatoes or pasta leaves our stomachs feeling full and our cravings satisfied.

Insoluble fiber is a good source of bulk, and helps relieve constipation and may decrease the risk of colon cancers.

Foods high in soluble fiber lower cholesterol levels. Oat bran is famous, of course, but a variety of other grains and vegetables are just as effective. Try barley, carrots, onions, soybeans, dried beans and peas, and oatmeal. In many studies, these foods have lowered cholesterol levels ten to twenty points in just three weeks, if eaten along with a low-fat diet. We learn more all the time about the health benefits of familiar, everyday foods.

PROTEIN   Most Americans eat too much protein! What do our bodies do with too much protein? They excrete it in the urine. Think about that the next time you eat an expensive steak!

Hamburgers, milk, cheese, steaks—our lives revolve around such high-protein (and high-fat) animal foods. Cut in half the amount of meat you eat, and eat more complex carbohydrates. Complex carbohydrates—dried beans, peas, rice, potatoes, and pasta—will provide ample protein, many other nutrients, and far less fat.

SODIUM   Sodium is a vital ingredient in our diets. But too much sodium increases the volume in the circulatory system and is a hazard for people with high blood pressure. For better health, learn to cook without salt and cut down on processed foods that are usually loaded with sodium.

ALCOHOL   Alcohol is high in calories and low in nutrients. Research shows that while one drink a day may actually be beneficial to lowering cholesterol levels, more can raise blood-pressure levels. No health professional would recommend anyone who does not already drink to start.

Help! Where to Go for Good Nutritional Advice

Where do you go for good nutritional advice? Before you do anything, pay a visit to your personal physician. Many physicians and other health authorities routinely refer their patients to registered dietitians (R.D.'s) who can translate the science of nutrition into a practical, everyday eating plan that fits *your* lifestyle (see Appendix B).

But no matter whose nutrition advice you take, make sure his or her professional credentials are related to nutrition and are *up to date*. Remember, you are paying for a valuable service and you want the best and most for your money, and your health.

Why Did I Call This Meeting? Oh Yes . . . the Microwave!

Remember that when you cook with the microwave, you will need less fat or no fat at all. The microwave retains vitamins and minerals as well as the best cooking methods, and in some vegetables the microwave retains more nutrients than other cooking methods. The microwave also intensifies the flavors of vegetables and many spices, so you can get along with less salt.

Your heart will be healthier without so much fat swimming throughout your blood vessels. But even with the microwave at the helm, you have to make some healthwise decisions on your own. You will see the three secrets[3] to a healthy meal often in this book. Learn the secrets

[3]Reprinted from the *American Cancer Society Cookbook* by Anne Lindsay (New York: Hearst Books, 1988).

now, for soon you will be putting them into practice—if you aren't already doing so. The secrets are found in:

1. The cuts of meats and other foods you buy
2. How you prepare them
3. How much of them you eat

Chapter 4 will help you with the first one by guiding your buying decisions. The recipes in this book will give you the key to the second. And number 3? Well, I make the recommendation, and the rest is up to you!

By now, you have plenty of reasons to take a healthy approach to cooking. Now, let's look at shopping tips, label reading, and how best to navigate your way around the grocery store to start with food destined to save your heart.

CHAPTER 3

Read That Label

ଔଔଔ

What the Label *Must* Tell Us

ଔ Who can make sense of the lingo on most food labels? Not many people, not even the secretary of health, education and welfare, who shortly after he assumed his position called supermarkets a "Tower of Babel." He said, "Consumers need to be linguists, scientists, and mind readers."

The Food and Drug Administration (FDA) and Congress are currently reviewing all label information in the hopes of making it easier to understand. Everything, from percentage of fruit juice in fruit-juice blends to how much meat should be in meat sauce, is under fire. But until any major legislation takes place, we're stuck with the label we have now.

In 1973, the FDA adopted regulations that led to the current nutrition label. (Except for fresh meats and alcoholic beverages, which are under the jurisdiction of other agencies, food labels must adhere to FDA regulations.)

The front of the label has to tell us:

- the name of the product and its form or style and packing medium, for example, "sliced pineapple packed in its own juice"
- the net weight of the food
- the name and address of the packer
- any special treatment, such as if the product has been evaporated or concentrated

INGREDIENT LIST

The nutrition panel, located on the back or side of the package, lists ingredients in descending order of predominance by weight, with the main ingredient listed first. In other words, if sugar is the first ingredient of a breakfast cereal and wheat flour is the second, you know immediately that the cereal contains more sugar than flour.

General, rather than scientific, language is permitted for most ingredients, such as fats, artificial colors and flavors. Yellow Dye No. 5 has to be specifically named because it causes allergic reactions in some people.

The label offers an eye-opening assortment of fats and sugars that food manufacturers use. Familiarize yourself with the names, because both fat and sugar comes in many guises. Dextrose, sucrose, corn syrup and corn-syrup solids, corn sugar, glucose, fructose, maltose, monosaccharides, sorbitol, or mannitol are all names of sugars.

The label will list the fats used. Fats that have been partially or completely hydrogenated will be stated on the label—soybean, corn, peanut, and safflower are some of the oils that may be partially hydrogenated. The label might include a clause that says "soybean, palm or cottonseed meal." This clause allows the manufacturer to use whichever fat he can buy cheaply.

STANDARDIZED FOODS

Exempt from the ingredient list are the ingredients in "standardized" foods, those adopted by the FDA for foods made with "standard" recipes. On these 350 foods, which include catsup, mayonnaise, milk, ice cream, cheese and macaroni, ingredients don't have to be printed on the label as long as manufacturers follow "approved" recipes. Optional ingredients do have to be listed.

THE NUTRITION PANEL

The nutrition panel may be located either on the back or side of food packages and includes (for each serving) the number of calories, grams of protein, carbohydrate, sodium, and fat. Also included are the percentage of the U.S. Recommended Daily Allowances (U.S. RDA)[1] for the essential nutrients protein, vitamin A, vitamin C, thiamin, riboflavin, niacin, calcium, and iron. If the product provides less than 2 percent of the U.S. RDA for any of these nutrients, a zero or asterisk will be listed after the nutrient. Twelve other optional nutrients, such as iodine, folic acid, and vitamin E, may be listed.

The percent of calories from fat, grams of cholesterol, and saturated and unsaturated fats are also optional on the nutrition panel.

---

[1] Set by scientists at the National Academy of Sciences, Committee on Dietary Allowances, Food and Nutrition Board. The Recommended Dietary Allowances (RDA) are the levels of intake of essential nutrients that, on the basis of scientific knowledge, are judged by the Food and Nutrition Board to be adequate to meet the known nutrient needs of practically all healthy persons.

Use this formula to determine the number of fat calories and the percentage of calories from fat in a food.

1. Multiply 9 (the number of calories in a gram of fat) times the number of grams of fat on the label. $9 \times 4 = 36$
2. Divide calories of fat (36) by total calories in a serving (155) $36 \div 155 = 23\%$

After a few practices, you will be able to pick up a package of almost any food and figure the percentage of fat.

LOWDOWN ON "LITE" FOODS

Advertisers tend to say the darndest things. If you shop for "lite" foods, you are a moving target for wide interpretation of the word "lite" or "light."

Does "lite" mean low in calories? Sometimes. Does "lite" mean low in sodium? Sometimes. Does it mean low in fat? Sometimes. And with one company, "lite" refers to the *color* of the food.

These are current regulations:[2]

FDA: The FDA regulates all processed foods and informally interprets "lite" to mean no more than forty calories per serving or no more than .4 calories for each gram of food. A "reduced calorie" claim must have at least 30 percent fewer calories than the regular product.

USDA: Meats and poultry products are regulated by the U.S. Department of Agriculture (USDA). The USDA requires a 25 percent reduction in calories, fat, sodium,

[2]Advocacy Update, May 1988, Public Voice for Food and Health Policy, a nonprofit consumer advocacy group in Washington, D.C.

breading, or other food component before it permits a "lite" claim. The nutrient that has been lowered must be identified. However, if a food has "lite" as part of the brand name, such as Lite Dinner Classics, the only requirement is that the package contain a nutrition label.

BATF: The Bureau of Alcohol, Tobacco, and Firearms (BAFT) has proposed that "lite" claims on alcoholic beverages be based on a 20 percent calorie reduction.

Now let's see how these laws work in real life: [3]

- Lipton's Oriental Vegetable Soup in its Lite Cup-a-Soup line has 40 calories per serving. Yet the Vegetable Soup flavor in Lipton's regular Cup-a-Soup line has only 35 calories per serving.
- A 4.5 oz. serving of Mrs. Paul's Ocean Perch Light Fillets contains 60 calories per ounce. Yet the Crispy Crunchy Breaded Fish, *not* marketed as "light," has 57 calories per ounce.
- Aunt Jemima Lite Syrup labels itself as having one half the calories of its regular syrup. But the regular syrup provides no calorie information and has no nutrition label.
- Weight Watcher's Chicken Enchiladas has 350 calories, 16 grams fat, 930 mg sodium. A shopper would assume this product would be light in *something,* but not to have 41 percent of the calories come from fat.

In other words, don't rely on the label to tell you as much as you would like to know. Let's hope future FDA regulations will be able to curb some of the wildest, most confusing claims.

---

[3] Information gathered directly from product labels from a supermarket in Atlanta, Georgia, in May 1990.

WHAT TO DO WITH FOODS THAT DON'T HAVE A NUTRITION LABEL

Foods that do not make a nutritional claim don't have to account for fat, cholesterol, calories, and other nutrients. What does this mean? Buyer beware! Always.

Bulk foods—simple foods such as potatoes and bananas don't have nutrition labels either—yet. That may change too, as the FDA reviews and adopts new rules.

The simpler a food is, the less that has been "done" to it, the more wholesome it is. Foods in their natural form have more nutrients and *much less* sodium than processed foods.

Look at the difference in nutrients between a simple baked potato and au gratin potatoes from a mix.

	Baked Potato w/Skin (one medium, 6-½ oz)	Au Gratin Potatoes (Mix) (1-cup serving)
Fat	0.2 gm. (0% U.S. RDA)	10 gm. (15% U.S. RDA)
Saturated Fat	0.1 gm. (0% U.S. RDA)	6.3 gm. (29% U.S. RDA)
Cholesterol	0	12 gm.
Sodium	16 mg. (1% U.S. RDA)	1076 mg. (49% U.S. RDA)
Vitamin C	26 mg. (43% U.S. RDA)	8 mg. (13% U.S. RDA)
Iron	2.7 mg. (23% U.S. RDA)	0.8 mg. (4% U.S. RDA)

Nutritive analysis from Michael Jacobson's Nutrition Wizard Software Program, © 1986, Center for Science in the Public Interest, 1875 Connecticut Ave., N.W., #300 Washington D.C. 20009.

Let's Go Shopping

Are you ready to show off your new knowledge in label reading? Then let's head to the store.

CHAPTER 4

Shopping

ഇ‍ഇ‍ഇ

Making Your List and Taking It on the Road

Incentives

GETTING STARTED OUT THE DOOR

ഇ Making up your mind to "eat better" is the first step toward better health. Only after you make that decision can you plan menus, grocery lists, and make smart decisions at the grocery store.

Good nutrition starts when you pick up a pen to write a grocery list. You look at menus. You look in your cupboards and refrigerator. And you *buy* what you need to make healthy dishes, such as the ones in this book. You are now, officially, out of excuses for not having a houseful of healthy foods.

As you walk the aisles, you will see vivid illustrations of how we kill the nutrition in perfectly healthy foods. For example, you can choose fresh apples, unsweetened or sweetened applesauce, sweetened apple cereal, or frozen apple pie. The only ingredient all of these foods have in common is the apples. The amounts of calories, sodium, and fat differ drastically. And making the right choices among the thousands of foods can mean the difference between your diet being a safeguard *against* heart disease or becoming a risk factor *for* heart disease.

From the previous chapter, you know about the U.S. Dietary Guidelines. These guidelines are the product of years of research, developed by teams of the most knowledgeable health professionals in the country.

Current research recommends we keep our diets:

Low in fat, sugar, salt, and alcohol
Moderate in protein
High in starches and complex carbohydrates

The recommendations sound great, don't they? But how do we put them in practice? The average person doesn't want to go to the grocery store with a calculator. Who in the world can figure out if 30 percent of his or her calories are coming from fat and 55 percent are coming from complex carbohydrates? "Do I have to measure every little bowl of oatmeal?" you ask.

And who can make out all the confusion in the grocery store?

For example: Did you know that bread wrappers are sometimes colored brown to make you think the bread inside is made from whole grain? Or that "meatballs" only have to be 65 percent meat? Just how healthy is prepackaged microwave popcorn? Is the fat in an avocado bad for you? How about salt-free potato chips? Is olive oil better than peanut or corn oil? Will oat-bran potato chips lower my cholesterol?[1]

[1]Answers to questions:
Popcorn: Not very.

These are typical questions for people who are trying to eat and shop to save their hearts. Shopping is a challenge to everyone. Grocery stores stock twenty thousand items these days, and you can't possibly know about all of them. Or what each food is made of, or how the food can fit into your family's menu. That's why the grocery store is still a good place to learn about nutrition—good and bad. The grocery store is where most people make their nutrition decisions.

BEFORE YOU LEAVE HOME

The best way to make good nutrition decisions is to be armed with a grocery list and meals planned in advance. *This is war.* If you are prepared, *you* will win. That way, you won't even have to wander down to enemy territory—the chips and cookie aisle.

Start your plans with the menus and recipes in the latter half of the book. They were developed with *you* in mind—you're in a hurry, like good food, *love* desserts, and want to eat healthfully without feeling deprived.

You don't have to buy three hundred dollars' worth of fresh food just to get started. Purchase food for your menus to last until your next shopping day. If you shop every day, buy only enough for one day. If you shop twice a

---

Avocado: The California avocado is 81 percent fat, but the fat is mostly monounsaturated and will not raise LDL cholesterol. The avocado is also high in many nutrients, so serve it, but serve it sparingly.
Salt-free potato chips: They may be salt-free, but they are still fried in old-fashioned oil. Don't bother.
Olive oil: Olive oil is mostly monounsaturated and is considered a healthy oil.
Oat-bran potato chips: Don't depend on them lowering your cholesterol. Read the package to see what ingredients were used to make them and what kind of fat was used to fry them. Remember, we're on a fat attack.

week, buy enough food to make the recipes for three or four days.

GROCERY-STORE TOURS

Before I tell you how to stake out your favorite store in order to save your heart, I want to alert you to a wonderful service that is available in many cities—grocery-store tours that are usually run by registered dietitians (R.D.'s). The tours will help you shop wisely, and healthfully, read a label, figure how many calories come from fat, and many other useful shopping tricks.

I'm going to give you a mini-tour right now, but to find out about bona fide tours in your city, call your own grocery-store manager, the food editor of your newspaper, or the local chapter of the American Dietetics Association (see Appendix B for national office address). Dial-a-Dietitian offers an information service in some communities.

The little money you will invest in the shopping tour will give you a bounty of information on nutrition, label reading, and healthy eating plans. And you can ask all the questions you need to.

NAVIGATING YOUR WAY AROUND
THE GROCERY STORE

When the U.S. Surgeon General made diet recommendations a few years ago, he made one strong statement: *eat simple foods.*

In order to eat a wholesome diet, you should choose the foods displayed around the perimeter of the grocery store—that's where you will often find the fresh fruits and vegetables, diary products, fresh meats, and bread. In other words, the *real* food. Ignore the prepared foods, junk foods, and candy—all the foods you don't need and probably have coupons for. Funny, companies never print discount coupons on fresh vegetables and whole grains.

The Well-Stocked Pantry (or How to Prevent Headache #9 at 6:00 P.M.)

Some ingredients should be in your pantry all the time—your staples. That way, you can pull together a meal whenever the need arises (like three times a day). I keep these foods around and use them constantly as I develop my Save Your Heart with Susan menus and recipes. The condiments especially are flavor-packed, so that you can avoid using an excess of salt and fatty foods for flavoring.

MY PANTRY

CONDIMENTS

Balsamic vinegar: This is an aged vinegar from Italy. Balsamic vinegar adds depth and intensity to dishes that might require beef stock or broth or fatty foods for flavoring—from chili to sauces. The vinegar is aged up to twenty-five years in wooden barrels made of chestnut, oak, juniper, or mulberry. The type of wood barrel is changed every year to add additional flavors. Like sun-dried tomatoes, balsamic vinegar is most easily found in specialty-food stores, and is unlike any other vinegar you have ever tasted.

Chicken stock: The flavor of chicken stock enhances so many recipes that it should always be available either in your freezer or on your shelf. Your homemade defatted stock will be the healthiest and most flavorful. If you must buy it, choose the lowest-sodium versions.

Mustards: Prepared mustards come in many varieties with many textures. They make a delicious addition to many dishes; just watch the sodium level in the products you buy. Dry mustard is another flavoring alternative.

Sun-dried tomatoes: These intensively flavored tomatoes add depth as well as flavor to many dishes. They come either dried or packed in olive oil. If you choose the ones in oil, remove them from the oil, blot off the extra, and cut them into slivers before adding to your dish.

FRESH AND DRIED HERBS As you take fat out of dishes, you will want to add flavor back, and herbs are an ideal way to add it. Fresh herbs not only provide better flavor than dried (with the exception of oregano, which is more intense when it is dried), but the color and texture of fresh herbs also add interest to many dishes.

Many herbs are easy to grow, and will keep you supplied at a moment's notice. (Of course, that's what all "herbies" say. Mine always died.)

Don't be afraid to try new herbs. The pungent flavorings are your friends—your bridge between reducing salt and fat in your diet and renewed health.

Most fresh herbs will keep for up to a week in the refrigerator (parsley is indestructible—it may last two weeks, while basil won't last even one). Leave fresh herbs unwashed, wrapped in a damp paper towel, and stashed in a plastic bag or other airtight plastic container. Dried herbs should be stored out of sunlight and in a coolish place. *Before using, crush herbs or rub them between your hands a bit to release the fragrance and flavor.*

Basil: Use this peppery, fresh-tasting herb in soups, tomato or grain dishes. Basil can be added to slow-cooking Italian sauces or served fresh over salads. Basils come in a variety of "flavors," such as cinnamon, anise, and lemon. Chop just before using. Fresh is best.

Bay leaf: An integral part of the French flavoring mixture bouquet garni, bay laurel adds a classic flavor to stews and soups. Bay needs gentle, long cooking to bring out its flavor. I often add more (three or four leaves) than recipes call for because it is a strong flavoring and a great substitute when cutting back on salt. Try it in chicken dishes.

Cilantro (fresh coriander or Chinese parsley): This refreshing lemon/peppery herb is used in Mexican and Chinese dishes, Indian curries and chutneys. The stems are an especially flavorful addition to simmering soups. Cut and use fresh cilantro in salsas and salads, add it to black bean soup or refried beans.

Chives: A mild species of the onion family. Snip these long tubular leaves and use them fresh on salads, baked potatoes, potato soup, steamed and sauced vegetables. I don't recommend dried chives; they become too strong-tasting to make an attractive garnish.

Dillweed: For potato salad or salmon, dill adds the right punch. The thin, delicate leaves can be snipped onto salads or other vegetables just before serving.

Garlic: A favorite of the onion family, fresh garlic adds to vinegars and salad dressings, but otherwise needs gentle cooking to bring out its flavor and aroma. I often cook garlic with oil or margarine as the first step in many dishes—it flavors the oil, softens the harsh flavor that garlic can have, and adds to the flavor of the dish.

Current research is taking a new look at garlic. Much folklore says garlic will cure everything from the common cold to cancer. So, just in case they are right, add garlic to your kitchen staples. More folklore says, A clove a day will keep your neighbors away. Just kidding, folks!

Marjoram: Sweet marjoram has a strong, aromatic scent and a more delicate flavor than its cousin oregan. Use it in salads, meats, grains, or vegetables. Dried marjoram has a more intense flavor than fresh, but add it toward the end of cooking to avoid losing the flavor.

Mints: From herbal tea to lemon mint rice, the sharp, refreshing flavor of mint adds pizzazz. Over five hundred varieties exist—from lemon to pineapple, apple to Italian peppermint. Mints are best served fresh or just barely cooked or steeped. Chop them just before using. Don't even consider using dried mint.

Oregano: Oregano is *the* familiar flavoring of pizza and spaghetti sauce. Dried or fresh, use oregano when it can be cooked for a little while to bring out its pungent flavor.

Parsley: This most overused but refreshing herb still has an important place in your kitchen. The curly kind we most often buy is more useful for garnishing than flavoring; the flat-leaf Italian parsley is the pungent one. Add it to soups, casseroles, sprinkle over vegetables or meats. The flat-leaf variety is especially useful when you are trying to cut back on salt.

Rosemary: Just rub your hands along a rosemary stem and smell the fragrance on your fingers. Ahhh . . . it's delightful, and the stiff, pinelike needles flavor roast chickens, lamb, soups, and stews. Stuff the stems and all into the cavity of a chicken, or snip off the needles for cooking and throw the woody stems on the grill or in the fireplace.

Sage: This strong-flavored herb is a member of the mint family. Sage is famous in Thanksgiving dressing (mine included), and in chicken and pork dishes. Dried sage becomes rancid and rank-tasting; store it in the freezer to preserve its delicate flavor.

Tarragon: French tarragon, the soul of béarnaise sauce, has a delicate anise flavor prized by the most skilled cooks. Used sparingly, it adds to stews, meats, and sauces, flavored vinegars, and mustards.

Thyme: The leaves of thyme are tiny but flavorful. Snip off the leaves for cooking and throw the woody stems into the fireplace. Thyme is wonderful in stews, poultry, and pork dishes, and salad dressings. The dozens of varieties include lemon, silver, caraway, and nutmeg—they all add significantly to a dish, especially as you take away the salt.

American Heart Association (AHA) spices: Salt-free spice combinations that come in handy when you are about to reach for the saltshaker.

FATS
Vegetable-Oil Margarine: Look for unsalted varieties. Make sure the first ingredient in the ingredient list is vegetable *oil.*

Olive Oil: Taking the fat out of food often means taking the flavor out too. The best counterattack is to make the fat you do use as packed with flavor as possible. Olive oil is a monounsaturated oil and considered one of the healthiest fats. Olive oils keep well if closed and protected from light in a cool cupboard.

The top grade—"extra-virgin"—comes from the gentle first pressing. It is a flavorful addition to salad dressings or other cold foods. "Extra-virgin" must also meet higher standards for flavor, color and aroma than are required of the lower grades. For cooking purposes, stick with the less expensive "virgin" or "pure" grades of olive oils; they have a higher smoke point and won't break down under heat.

Canola oil: The newest oil to hit the shelves, canola oil, like olive oil, is a monounsaturated oil. The flavor is very bland and is useful in cooking and baking when you don't want the pungent flavor of olive oil.

Other specialty oils: Walnut, sesame, hazelnut, are all unrefined and wonderful oils to use in small doses on fresh greens for a small but flavor-packed punch. Use them tossed with steamed vegetables, or in salads and other uncooked preparations as you would extra-virgin olive oil.

Peanut oil: This useful oil is mostly monounsaturated and has a high smoke point. Some brands are much more flavorful than others, so "taste around." (And don't just stick with the big companies; some small companies, such as Loriva, are producing delicious oils.)

Other oils: Corn, safflower, sunflower, soybean oil—these polyunsaturated oils are the "regulars" in the kitchen. They are tasteless; their best uses are in baking and cooking rather than on salads.

SOME KITCHEN STAPLES
Grains and Beans

White Rice: Long-grain converted rice is the most nutritious white rice. Also look for the naturally flavorful basmati, Texmati (basmati grown in Texas), pecan, and jasmine rices. The long grain produces drier, fluffier rice and short grain produces a stickier rice, useful if you are using chopsticks.

Brown rice: This whole-grain rice also comes in long and short grain.

Wild rice/long-grain rice boxed together: Throw out the spice packet as it is high in sodium.

Pasta: Spaghetti, fettuccine, macaroni. Imported brands have better flavor and firmer texture.

Bulgur: A cracked-wheat product with a nutty flavor. It's precooked, so it cooks quickly like precooked rice products, but is much more delicious.

Wheat germ: Toasted wheat germ has a nutty flavor that makes a nice addition when sprinkled on foods. Refrigerate after opening.

Oatmeal

Bran flakes cereal

Oat bran: Process oat bran in the food processor for finer-textured baked goods.

Dried beans: Great northern, navy, cranberry, black, kidney, red, pinto, black-eyed peas and cowpeas are just some of the delicious beans to choose from.

Dried lentils: Green, orange, or yellow are interchangeable in recipes.

Corn meal: Choose stone-ground whole grain if possible, as it retains more vitamins and minerals. You may need to go to a health-food store for this. Keep stone-ground cornmeal in the refrigerator or freezer to prevent the fat from becoming rancid.

Cake flour: Because of its lower protein (gluten), it's the flour of choice for baking in the microwave.

Whole-wheat flour: Choose stone-ground if possible. Refrigerate it to prevent the fat from becoming rancid. Lower in gluten than all-purpose flour.

All-purpose flour: Because of its higher protein (gluten) it will tend to toughen microwave-baked products.

Cornstarch: This will help thicken sauces and stabilize yogurt cheese before cooking.

Vegetables
Yellow onions: Best for slow cooking in stews and casseroles. Sweet onions are generally available only when in season. Vidalias, for example, are available only in early summer. (Because new storage techniques are being developed, we may be able to enjoy them even longer.)

White onions: Use in Mexican cooking, both cooked and raw preparations.

Green onions (scallions)

Leeks: These require long, gentle cooking for exquisite onion flavor. Add to soups and stews.

Bell peppers: Green, red, yellow, and brown—a great staple. The reds are sweeter.

Tomatoes, canned: Choose the lowest-sodium you can find.

Whole tomatoes

Tomato sauce

Tomato paste

Tomatoes with chilies

Catsup

Dairy Products
Butter substitutes: These powders can be used to shake on foods to add butter flavoring—to popcorn and baked potatoes.

Egg substitutes: Egg substitutes are best disguised in baking, where the texture and "look" of a "real" egg won't be an issue. They are also great for omelets. Different brands are available, and some taste better than others, so try all brands. They contain no cholesterol but they have more fat than plain egg whites.

Low-fat sour cream: A perfect topper for baked potatoes. Mix with nonfat yogurt to lower the fat even more.

Low-fat cottage cheese: A taste alternative.

Low-fat cheddar cheese: A low-fat version of a familiar cheese. You may not notice the difference, but your blood vessels will!

Nonfat dry milk: Great for thickening sauces or adding body to skim milk when the family balks.

Nonfat yogurt: Use this to make yogurt cheese (see page 333).

Part-skim ricotta cheese: A delicious alternative, and I bet you won't be able to tell the difference.

Skim milk, one-half-percent fat: The lowest-fat, lowest-calorie milk is the best for your heart. Drink it and cook with it.

Evaporated skim milk: This tastes and cooks just like the other evaporated milk. The skim-milk version is a great way to cut fat and calories in everything from pumpkin pie to sauces to casseroles. It is a star ingredient in my recipe Marie's Chicken Casserole.

Fresh eggs: You'll be using a lot of egg whites. Free-range or brown eggs may have a more assertive flavor depending on the chicken's diet, but the nutritional breakdown is the same. Don't waste money on "low-cholesterol" eggs—new testing procedures show that *all* eggs are lower in cholesterol than a decade ago.

Some Old and New Products: A Glossary and Editorial

Ground turkey: Turkey is very low in saturated fat and cholesterol. To get the lowest-fat ground turkey, request ground breast meat. Fresh or frozen prepackaged turkey usually has the skin (and fat) ground in with the meat.

"Natural" meat: "Natural" is a wide category and has a different meaning to different meat producers. Some companies are raising animals with no hormones or antibiotics. Some feed the animals only organic grains or allow the animals free range rather than a restrictive environment. Others are feeding cattle on grasses or grains that are lower in fat (and flavor) than corn, to produce lower-fat meat. Some of the meats are fine products, and some I can't get past the first bite. Follow your tastebuds and your conscience, but be sure to read the label to see what "natural" refers to.

In general the "natural" meats have a firmer texture because they are lower in fat. Beef items usually require longer, slower cooking to break down the connective tissue. Free-range chickens, available in some health-food stores, may also require longer cooking, but the flavor of these chickens is superb—just like the chickens Grandma used to eat. And remember, a more flavorful chicken will require less seasoning.

Wild game: Americans are increasingly turning to game— from venison and rabbit to pheasant and quail—as a very low-fat source of protein. The assertive flavors of game can be just the answer for people working to cut dietary salt.

Cholesterol-free engineered meats and other low-fat products: If you like the taste of these, note the amount of fat and figure it into your new healthy eating plan. I would personally rather give up bacon forever (that's a long time) than to eat imitation bacon. The sausage patties are better.

"Fat substitutes" are destined to be big sellers, adding the mouth-feel of fat without the calories or associated health problems. Ice cream, sour cream, cake mixes, and fried foods such as French fries are expected targets for fat substitutes.

With fat substitutes, don't assume you can gorge on fat without consequences. Fat substitutes are expected to lower fat intake only by about 5 percent. You will still need to make a variety of healthy food choices. Remember, sugar substitutes did not make us thin!

Salt-free potato chips: Save your money. You'll be getting a hefty dose of fat because the chips are fried. Try pretzels instead.

Other salt-free products: Many foods now come unsalted or with reduced sodium, such as broth, tomatoes and other vegetables, soups and sauces. Keep these stocked on your shelves. While some canned beans and other vegetables can be drained and rinsed to remove excess sodium, rinsing is impossible with stocks and soups.

Frozen dinners: Most frozen dinners are loaded with fat and sodium. You *must* read the labels. Even dinners that are calorie controlled may have too much fat and sodium.

Many companies have made a genuine effort to produce a complete line of frozen dinners that comply with the U.S. Dietary Guidelines. Le Menu Light Style, Healthy

Choice, and Right Choice are three examples. The nutrition information is easy to find and clearly stated. Hats off to these companies: Campbell's, ConAgra, and Stouffer's.

"Diet" foods/ersatz foods: Why don't people want to eat *real food?* Why do "foods" have to be engineered and biodeveloped and formulated? Why make our lives any more complicated than they already are? If you choose to buy these foods, *read the labels.* If a food is called "diet" or "low cholesterol" it could also just as easily be full of fat and sodium. Buyer beware. Always.

Getting to the Nitty-Gritty of Saving Your Heart

LOOKING FOR FAT IN ALL THE RIGHT PLACES
Compare the fat, saturated fat, and cholesterol in the following foods to help you make good save-your-heart food choices.

Food	Amount raw weight	Fat gm	Sat fat gm	Cholesterol mg
Beef, Ground, Reg.	3 oz.	18	6.9	76
Beef Liver, Fried	3 oz.	7	2.5	410
Beef, Roast	2.8 oz	8	2.7	75
Chicken with Skin	3 oz.	15.3	4.3	184
Chicken w/out Skin	3 oz.	2.9	0.8	136
Chicken Liver	2 livers	2.0	0.8	252
Turkey, Roasted	1 cup	7.0	2.3	106
Hot dog	1 frank	13	4.8	23
Lamb, Leg Roasted	2.6 oz.	6	2.4	65
Veal	3 oz.	9	4.1	86
Fish (Flounder)	3 oz.	1	0.3	59
Shrimp	4 oz.	1.2	.2	171
Butter	1 tbsp.	11	7.1	31

Food	Amount raw weight	Fat gm	Sat fat gm	Cholesterol mg
Whole Egg	1 large	5	1.5	213
Skim Milk	1 cup	0.4	.3	4
Whole Milk	1 cup	8	5.1	33
Cheddar Cheese	1 oz.	9	6.0	30
Low-fat Cheddar	1 oz.	5		200
Nonfat Yogurt	1 cup	0.4	0.3	4
Sour cream	1 tbsp.	3	1.6	5
Ice cream, 11% Fat	1 cup	14	8.9	59
Oatmeal, Cooked	1 cup	2	0.4	0
Potatoes	1 baked	0.2	0.1	0
Rice, Brown	1 cup	1.0	0.3	0

Nutritive analysis from Michael Jacobson's Nutrition Wizard Software Program, © 1986, Center for Science in the Public Interest, 1875 Connecticut Ave., N.W., #300, Washington, D.C. 20009. Egg figures from the Georgia Egg Commission.

You can find fat in plenty of other places. Keep trimming!

AT THE MEAT COUNTER (TRIM THE FAT AND FATTEN YOUR PURSE)

1. Cut your meat consumption. Meat is filled with "hidden fat," such as that in steaks. Serve smaller portions less often.

2. Eat more lean cuts of meat, whether from beef, veal, pork, chicken, turkey or fish. Trim off as much visible fat and skin as possible.

Beef is graded by fat content. "Choice," the highest grade you can buy in the grocery store, has the highest fat content. "Select" is next, and will be a healthier choice. These meats may require longer, slower cooking methods to bring out their tenderness and flavor.

In beef: Choose lean round steak, top round, flank steak,

lean ground round (about 15 percent fat), and rump. The amount of fat required in ground round, chuck, and ground hamburger varies from state to state, and more than half the states *do not* require a fat limit or a fat label.

In pork: Choose the tenderloin or center loin, fresh leg, cubed steak, lean center ham cuts, and Canadian bacon. Today's pork is much leaner than a decade ago, and much of it meets the U.S. Dietary Guidelines.

3. Don't buy high-fat meats such as bologna, salami, bacon, and hot dogs, even if they are made from turkey or chicken.

AT THE DAIRY CASE

1. Use low-fat or non-fat items such as milk, sour cream, and yogurt.

2. Use unsalted margarine rather than butter, and buy only those that list "vegetable oil" as the first ingredient.

ADDING THE FIBER

CARBO-LOADING FOR EVERYONE!

1. Eat five fruits and vegetables every day, raw whenever possible. One health authority suggested making sure every day's diet had "three colors and crunch."

2. Eat the skin of fruits and vegetables, such as apples and potatoes, whenever possible.

3. Choose to eat fruit rather than drink fruit juice.

4. Choose breads, cereals, and crackers made of whole grain rather than refined grains.

5. Cut sugar and other sweeteners to a minimum.

WHERE TO FIND DIETARY FIBER

Cereals and Breads	Serving Size	Grams Dietary Fiber[1]
Oat Bran	⅓ cup dry	2.0*
All-Bran	⅓ cup dry	10.00*
Rice Bran*	⅓ cup dry	6.00
Oatmeal*	⅔ cup, cooked	2.7*
Wonder High Fiber Wheat	2 slices	5.8
Pepperidge Farm 5-Star Fiber Apple Spice	2 slices	6.0*
Dried Beans, Peas, and Rice		
Black-eyed Peas	¾ cup, cooked	12.3*
Kidney Beans	¾ cup, cooked	13.8*
Pinto Beans	¾ cup, cooked	14.2*
Navy Beans	¾ cup, cooked	9.0*
Lentils	¾ cup, cooked	5.6*
Split Peas	¾ cup, cooked	4.1*
Brown Rice	1 cup, cooked	3.3
Converted White Rice	1 cup, cooked	1.0
Vegetables		
Baked Potato w/skin	1 medium	4.2*
Peas, canned	½ cup, cooked	2.9
Corn	½ cup, cooked	3.1
Sweet potato w/out skin	1 baked	3.4*
Summer Squash	½ cup, cooked	1.1
Cauliflower	½ cup, cooked	1.4
Broccoli	½ cup, cooked	2.0
Carrot, raw	1	2.3*
Fruit		
Prunes	5	3.5*
Pears	1	4.3
Apples w/skin, large	1	4.7*
Bananas, medium	1	1.8
Oranges	1	3.1*

[1] Total dietary fiber figures are given because not all foods have been measured separately. When a significant amount of soluble fiber is present (at least a gram) that food is noted with an asterisk *.

Selected foods taken from "Rough It Up," fiber chart, 1990, Center for Science for the Public Interest, 1875 Connecticut Ave., NW, #300, Washington, D.C. 20009, $5.00.

Adapting Recipes

I know you have recipes you don't want to give up. I understand—I didn't want to give up cheesecake or strawberry pie or chocolate pudding either. The best part is, I *didn't* give them up; I adapted these recipes.

You don't have to take *everything* out of a recipe to make it heart-healthy. Believe me, I'm not into suffering. A little cut here and little cut there will usually be enough to bring your fat intake in line. See Appendix C for some substitutions.

To cut the fat, sodium, and calories in recipes, you either have to change the method you use or change the ingredients.

Microwaving rather than sautéing is a healthier way to cook. Ingredient amounts can be lowered or omitted, depending on how important the ingredient is to the success of the recipe.

In the following recipe, for example, the sugar was cut in half. Halving the sugar wouldn't be possible in cake recipes, but here it wasn't as crucial. Half the sugar will do fine. Many times salt can be omitted entirely, or herbs used as a replacement with no reduction of flavor or texture. You may discover a better flavor. Experiment and be creative.

Let's take one of my favorite "old-fashioned" recipes, one for chocolate pudding. It's luscious, rich, and high in fat. I want to show you how, with just a few minor alterations, it became "No Guilt" Chocolate Pudding, one of my most-requested TV recipes (see page 176). Total grams of fat are shown for each recipe, then the calories from fat in each recipe.

Save-Your-Heart-Style	Fat (gm)	Old-Style	Fat (gm)
⅓ cup sugar	0	Twice as much sugar	0
2 tablespoons cocoa	2.0	Chocolate squares	14.6
1 tablespoon cornstarch	0	No change	0
1 cup skim milk	.4	Whole milk	8
2 egg whites	0	Whole egg or egg yolks	6
1 teaspoon margarine	3.5	2 tablespoons butter	11
½ teaspoon vanilla	0	No change	
	5.4		39.6

Multiply the grams of fat by 9 calories each:
or 49 fat calories   or 360 fat calories

Is "No Guilt" Chocolate Pudding looking better to you?

The next chapter will give you expert directions to buying the perfect microwave. You are on your way to the healthiest, most delicious cooking ever.

CHAPTER 5

The Microwave Oven

ଓଡ଼ଓ

Making Choices

THE BEST ZAPPER OF THEM ALL

ଓ Over 80 percent of Americans now own a microwave oven. No doubt about it, the convenience and the ease of cooking in the microwave has changed the way America cooks.

You may be one of those 80 percent. You may be an old hand at cooking in the microwave or you may be rather new at it. Either way, this chapter may teach you a thing or two.

If you are searching for that perfect machine, limitless possibilities await you. This chapter may teach you more about what you *already have!*

You want a microwave you will *use,* so you have to be comfortable with all its gadgets, dials, and dings.

Is the fan quiet? Do the beeps drive you mad? Is the light inside bright enough to see the food easily, and is the light bulb easy to replace, or does it even matter? (One company touts how easy changing the light bulb is in their microwave. However, theirs is the only microwave light bulb that I ever had to stock in my store—they burned out constantly!) These are just a few seemingly minor details that might bring you satisfaction with your microwave oven or drive you away. So read the following information carefully.

After many years in the retail microwave and cooking-school business, I feel secure in guiding you toward the best options and sizes, and away from those that might just waste your money. I didn't just sell microwaves, I *cooked* with them every day, and *taught* cooking classes using them to cook! real food! from scratch! and eat it! Imagine.

How much do I use my microwave ovens? (You notice I said that in plural.) To give you an idea, I dust that "other" stovetop in my kitchen every couple of weeks, just to see if it's still there. (In case I ever want to sell the house, a cooktop would be helpful.) The oven in the "other" stove is also a great storage spot. I used to hide Tex's birthday present in it, knowing it was a place he would *never* think to look.

If you buy the right microwave oven for your needs, you will use yours just as much as I use mine. If you don't, it will be a constant source of irritation.

Ten years ago, people bought microwaves that defrosted meat and cooked food on high, period. Since then, the lineup of options has exploded. The list now includes everything from small-sized, low-priced microwaves to full-featured, computerized machines that do almost everything for you.

And options once considered top of the line, such as turntables and temperature probes, can be found on the most pedestrian of models. These are just some of the topics we will explore in this chapter and the next.

First, Let's Look at the Basics.

I'M COOKING WITH RADIO WAVES?
COME ON . . .

That's right. Microwaves are nothing more than short, high-frequency electromagnetic waves that fall somewhere between radio and light waves in frequency or length. A magnatron tube (the heart of the microwave) inside the microwave oven converts electricity into microwaves. When these "waves" touch water, fat, or sugar in foods (they like these foods best, like some of us), they cause movement, or friction, of those molecules in the food. As the molecules move, they cause heat, much like when you rub your hands together on a cold day. And because the microwaves are short and high frequency, they move *fast,* causing the food to heat *fast.* And then they fade away just as fast. It's that simple. And that safe.

Since microwaves travel in a straight line, they have to be distributed and patterned. The method of distributing microwave energy within the cavity of the microwave is so important that I have left that discussion to a separate section later in this chapter. Please read it carefully. Even cooking will make the difference between making microwave cooking a joy or a joke.

And I want to clear one thing up right now. I just think you should have the right idea about how the microwaves cook food. Microwaves penetrate the first inch or so of food, and the heat produced then travels toward the center of the food and continues to cook by old-fashioned heat conduction—from the outside to the inside. *Food does not cook from the inside out.*

WHAT IF I DON'T LIKE IT?

Don't you hate to buy a pig in a poke? Of course you do. So before you purchase the machine, find out if you will be allowed to return it if it isn't just what you wanted. To find out if you chose the right machine, sign up for some microwave-cooking classes. Experience tells me that you will benefit more if you take the classes *after* you buy the microwave; that way, you can rush home after each class and put your machine through its paces. But for heaven's sake, take some classes! Some stores will even offer free classes—my store always did.

I also know if you take classes you will *use* your new microwave a hundred times more than someone who doesn't take classes. I realize these classes may not be available where you live. That's why I've provided basic cooking lessons in Chapters 8 and 9. These two chapters are crammed full of some of the same information I teach in my Beginning Microwave class.

DO I OR DON'T I?

Do I want a thermostat or multiple programming? A browner or sensor that *tells* me when my food is cooked? Do I want to hang the microwave under a cabinet, or do I only have room to set it on a cart in the hallway?

Don't expect to know exactly what you will need when you walk into the store. You probably won't know your full needs until you have used the microwave awhile and have actually tried some recipes (mine, I hope.) A microwave is not like a dishwasher—with those machines people generally know what to ask for. But with the (still) newfangled microwave, many of the options available are confusing—and some, not particularly useful. The following pages will detail most of the available options and accessories. I hope this information will ease the confusion and make your decision an easier one.

PRIORITIES

You are now in the microwave department of your favorite store, standing in front of rows and rows of microwaves. You're in a cold sweat looking at the huge selection. The salesperson is walking toward you. Now take a deep breath and listen to the sales "pitch." You need to decide if the salesperson is interested in *your* needs or his or hers. You know what to do in either case. I am including the questions I asked my customers when I helped them choose the right microwave for their lifestyle.

First of all, I would look for the biggest, most even-cooking, least expensive microwave to fit their space. That space might be twenty inches in width or three feet. Each person's situation is different, as is the way each person eats. So I had to know about the customer's lifestyle first to find the perfect fit with a microwave. I had a huge selection of microwaves because of different customer needs. If your store has only two or three to choose from, try another store.

The priorities are divided into seven categories to speed you along. These priorities are *mine*. *Your* seven might be different. You may look at the list and say, "Buying American is my first priority," or "I only want the brand I work for." These are legitimate requirements. The point is, *know yours*. The following are the ones I think are most important.

1. Placement	Where will it go?
2. Size	How much space do you have? What do you eat, and how many people are eating?
3. Even cooking	Crucial to successful cooking. Look at different methods of distributing microwave energy.

4. Wattage   This will affect cooking times and partly depends on size of microwave.

5. Power levels How many are adequate?

6. Features   What can the microwave "do"?

7. Manufacturer Who, what, and where. Do you care?

Darling, Where Shall We Put It?

FINDING THE RIGHT SPOT

Before you leave home, decide where you plan to put the microwave—on a counter, perhaps. Better yet, choose two spots. Measure the height, width, and depth of both spaces. Your salesperson will give you much better service when you come prepared!

You can hang the microwave under a cabinet, set it on a counter or cart, build it into a wall, or hang it over your range. All four are perfect options—it just takes the right type of microwave, space, and possibly a professional appliance installer to help if you can't do it yourself.

I'm not going to spend much time on the subject of setting the microwave on a counter or cart; I will say that the microwave should be placed where it will be convenient for you to use, not halfway across the basement or in a utility closet. I realize you are now into exercise, but this doesn't apply.

If you already know you are setting your microwave on a counter or cart, skip to page 71. If not, read on.

HANG IT, DANG IT

Manufacturers produce two types of microwaves that are capable of being hung in place: ones that fit over the stove or range with a built-in vent and light, and those that can fit under a cabinet.

Both types have some space requirements, as well as some "people" requirements.

First, a remark about size: about yours, that is. You (or the main microwave operator) must be tall enough to see into the microwave, and not risk pulling hot containers into your face. Placing the microwave too high would be a safety hazard and is not recommended. And don't forget about the size of children who might be using the microwave. Can they reach it? You do want them to learn to cook, don't you?

BEHIND DOOR #1 . . .

I own one of these "over-the-range" microwaves and love it for several reasons. It's at eye level, and off the counter. Also, the microwave takes up space that only an ugly hood would use, and the microwave has its own built-in light and ventilation fan, which was the purpose of the hood anyway. But don't try to hang just any type of microwave oven above the range—unless the microwave has been specially designed, it won't be able to handle the extra heat and moisture that wafts up from the cooktop, and it won't be wide enough.

If you want to install a microwave above your stove or range, you will need a space of 30 inches from the burners on your stove to the bottom of the cabinet above your stove. (Don't include the hood in this figure, if you currently have one.)

You will also need a minimum of 30 inches in width—in other words, the width of your stove. If you have more than 30 inches, or up to 42 inches, that's fine too. If the space is more than 30 inches, "spacers" or "filler" panels can be installed on either side of the microwave.

If you don't like the look of the plain panels, a carpenter could easily make panels to match the wood of your cabinets. The people who sell you your "over-the-range" microwave should have (or should order) the filler panels for you. If they don't or won't, take your business to a store that will.

You need to know if you presently vent your cooking top outside or inside your kitchen. Some over-the-range microwaves can recirculate cooking fumes inside your kitchen through a charcoal filter. The charcoal filter is sold separately, is inexpensive, and lasts at least a year. All over-the-ranges can be vented to the outside.

For stability, these over-the-range microwaves attach to the studs in the wall behind your stove, and are anchored with bolts in the cabinet above the stove. Even so, make sure *your* cabinets can handle the sixty-five or more pounds that most of these microwaves weigh. Although the wall studs will handle most of the weight, the cabinets will share the load.

A tip I learned the hard way at installation time is this: Cover the burners of your stove with plastic or a sheet to keep the dust from settling in them. I didn't, and I wish I had. (You can guess how much I like to clean).

AND BEHIND DOOR #2 . . .

Other microwaves with names like "Under the Cabinet," "Spacesaver," or "Hanging," fit beautifully under kitchen cabinets.

Under-the-cabinet models are usually about 12 inches deep to match the depth of most cabinets. The crucial test is the height of the microwave oven you want and the space available under your cabinets. Check this space before you buy just any old hanging microwave.

Some math will help: Kitchen cabinets are usually hung from 15 inches to 21 inches above the countertops. Therefore, if you have a 9-inch-tall microwave oven, and your cabinets are 21 inches from the counter, you have exactly 12 inches—a foot—of usable space under your microwave. Is that enough space for you to handle your usual countertop chores? A foot of space would be adequate for me. It might not be for you.

Perhaps your cabinets are hung only 15 inches above your countertops. That same 9-inch "space saver" microwave would leave you only 6 inches for countertop chores. Yes, you could call that a spacesaver, but space saved for what? If the space is limited from countertop to cabinet bottom, you could be better off setting the microwave directly on the counter.

Don't forget the price of brackets to hold the microwave in place. In the good old days, they were usually thrown in the deal for free. It's happening less and less, so ask. And remember, since microwave prices are getting lower and lower, manufacturers are cutting costs any way they can.

BUILDING IN AND TRIMMING

The advantage of many microwaves is that they can be "built-in" and "trimmed" to look as if they were part of the kitchen cabinetry. These are really just "regular" microwave ovens that would normally sit on a counter, but to give the kitchen a finished look, or to save counter space, they are often built-in, perhaps above a conventional wall oven or among the cabinets. Kitchen designers and remodelers often work to give the microwave the same finished look of other appliances, as it ties the kitchen together.

But microwaves come in a variety of widths, from a petite 18 inches to a full 24 inches. Survey the width of your available space before choosing a microwave oven. That way it will fit into your overall design.

"CUTOUT" DIMENSIONS

For microwaves that are to be built-in or trimmed, you will need to know certain dimensions, called "cutout" dimensions to accommodate the venting and space around the microwave. These dimensions will depend on the model you choose, as microwaves vent from the front, top, or back.

Building in a microwave with a trim kit is a project usually best left to a professional. Trim kits can be ordered directly from a company called Micro-Trim (see Appendix E), or from the dealer where you bought your microwave. Some manufacturers, such as Amana, General Electric, Magic Chef, Panasonic, Quasar, and Sharp, manufacture trim kits to accommodate specific models. The trim kits are usually dark brown, black, or white, and have matching grillwork to allow proper venting. The manufacturer trim kits are usually available for two or three years after the microwave model year. Older microwaves may need custom-built kits.

Many mass merchandisers who sell a lot of microwave ovens won't have heard of trim kits. Some retailers will special order a trim kit for you. If not, call Micro-Trim directly.

ELECTRICITY GREASES THE WHEEL

Make sure your chosen space has electrical outlets nearby. You will need a grounded outlet (or a three-prong outlet) to accommodate any microwave. All noncommercial microwaves work from 110 to 120 volts and 60 cycles, just like your coffeepot and toaster. And please, no extension cords.

A microwave works best if it has its own "dedicated circuit," away from refrigerator plugs and other appliances.

Why do you want a dedicated circuit for your microwave? Because you don't want your microwave to have to share "power" with another appliance. Sharing power may affect the cooking time of your food. Too many appliances sharing a circuit may also blow a fuse. (I have a friend who didn't heed my advice on this, and at night she has learned to microwave in the dark—if she turns on the kitchen light, the circuit is overloaded.) And don't assume that if your microwave oven is the only appliance plugged into the receptacle that it has its own circuit—sometimes one circuit will supply several wall receptacles. Ask your electrician.

You may also notice that food takes longer to cook in the microwave at certain times of the day, such as at dinnertime when everyone else is cooking dinner, or at certain times of the year. And summer cooking may take longer because of the power drain from air conditioners—it's a bit like trying to wash dishes, clothes, and the dog all at the same time—all you will get from the faucet will be a trickle of water.

What is happening? You're just getting less power into your house. It has nothing to do with the quality of your microwave. Just plan on a little extra cooking time.

Which Microwave Is Right for Me?

BUYER BEWARE

If you've ever shopped for an appliance or an electronic anything, you know how easy it is to be overwhelmed by rows and rows of machines. I know I have. I have also said to Tex, on our way to the store, "We're not going to spend more than fifty dollars for the robot that cleans house and washes clothes," knowing full well that we probably will. To make you feel better, I have also found that I used to underbuy and ended up wishing I had purchased the upgraded model after all. So remember, in microwave shopping, it's usually better to seemingly overbuy. A few extra features won't cost much more, and you'll soon "grow into them."

I didn't want "buyer's remorse"[1] to set in on my customers, so I always gave them sixty days to exchange their microwave for another one. They could go up or down in

---

[1] Second-guessing yourself after you have purchased something—a car, house, dress, or even a pet.

features and price in that time period and receive full credit. Ninety-nine out of a hundred times, customers traded up if they decided to exchange one microwave for another. So ask your salesperson for the same exchange privilege. After all, a *good* microwave oven should last for eight or ten years.

I WANT TO TRAVEL ON A BOAT, NOT COOK IN ONE.

If you like reading computer-software manuals and figuring your income tax, you should find the maze of microwave-oven sizes just fascinating.

Believe it or not, microwave-oven sizes and model names may have little to do with how they look on the outside. The interior size is what matters. The insides are measured by cubic-foot capacity, which means height times length times depth. And, of course, microwave ovens have no "official" size or shape categories. You don't think the manufacturers would make it *that* easy for us, do you?

Square-shaped models will provide more headroom, but possibly not enough width to set a couple of healthy frozen dinners side by side. And the low and wide models might accommodate two full-sized dinner plates, but won't take a popcorn popper or casserole more than five inches high. So check your space requirements before you go shopping.

The lesson is, don't buy a microwave by its name (or because it's cute). The microwave you love might be called "Family Size," but one look inside could prove it wrong. It might be better suited to store your shoes in.

What is the secret formula to buying a microwave oven? Try to buy a microwave with the smallest *exterior* and the largest *interior*.

WILL MY DOG DISH WORK?

Many of the dishes you cook in now may work fine in the microwave too—you can find out with a dish-test in Chapter 7.

In determining the best size microwave for you, keep in mind the size dishes you like to use. For example, if you *always* use a 9 × 13-inch baking dish to prepare Swiss Steak, or if you have a big family and always cook in quantity, buying a microwave that will only accommodate a dinner plate would not make sense.

The Lowdown on Microwave Sizes—My Definitions

To ease the confusion, we're going to create our own "official" Save Your Heart with Susan size categories. This is going to be fun.

- Full Size
- Midsize
- Compact
- Subcompact
- Never Mind

EVERYTHING BUT THE KITCHEN SINK: FULL SIZE

Full-size microwaves range in size from 1.2 to 1.5 cubic feet and usually have 700 to 800 watts.

Because of the high wattage in full-size microwaves, foods cook faster than in lower-wattage ones.

Of course, full-size microwaves often come loaded with

extra features and will accommodate the largest pans, the tallest popcorn popper, the juiciest turkey.

THE MIDDLEWEIGHT CHAMP: MIDSIZE

These microwaves range from .8 to 1.1 cubic feet, and have 600 to 700 watts. Many of them will accommodate a 9″ × 13″ baking dish or a three-quart casserole. If you have particular dishes you like to use, take them along when you shop.

Midsize microwaves can come loaded with features and accessories too.

LA PETITE: COMPACT

Compact microwaves range from .6 to .7 cubic feet and most have 600 watts. It is the size I usually use when I'm cooking on TV (see the story on my life as a TV "Star," page 139). The compact is an excellent size for an "extra" machine, which I think should be in every kitchen!

For Erin, a newlywed, it is a perfect size. Just remember, you don't want to be constantly transferring leftovers into smaller containers—that's not convenient. So don't underbuy, size-wise.

IT'S-CUTE-AND-IT-COOKS-TOO?

These microwaves are .4 or .5 cubic feet, usually 500 watts and often come equipped with a 10″ × 10″ glass tray, and most will hold a dinner plate. I recommended this size for Erica, for college.

SMALLER THAN A BREAD BOX: NEVER MIND

Can I say anything nice about a microwave oven that has 300 watts and is one third (.3) of a cubic foot in size and only cooks on high?

No!

Strategies for Even Cooking

A HISTORY LESSON

The earliest microwaves were miserable creatures with very uneven cooking. The excited new microwave owners soon found that after cooking, one side of their food would be cold and the other would have cooked to a rock—that's because microwaves travel in a straight line, and somehow they have to be distributed throughout the inside of the microwave oven. The early machines had terrible microwave-energy distribution systems.

The obvious next step was to tell these eager consumers that they had to turn their food every minute or so. Now that's convenient! Finally, some smart person decided to put the food on a turntable and let it spin the food. Sounds good, eh? Unfortunately, it wasn't that simple.

Patterning or distributing microwaves for even cooking has evolved and improved over the years.

And now, to *the* most important criterion for choosing a microwave after you have determined the size you want to buy: Does the microwave cook evenly without your having to turn the food?

STIRRER FANS IN THE FLOOR, BOTTOM FEED

The best method of distributing microwaves is a "hidden" stirrer fan under the floor of the microwave. The turntable *effect* is there, without the inflexibility of the turntable itself. This hidden-stirrer-fan, bottom-fed system, distributes the microwaves extremely well so that food cooks and defrosts evenly.

I like this system best because I rarely have to "turn" my food, and because the turntable is under the floor of the microwave, any dish will fit. This style microwave is easier to clean. You'll never know if the microwave-distribution system is "bottom feed" if you don't ask, and salespeople usually don't think to tell you.

I've had this design of microwave for years because of its even cooking, reasonable price, and convenience. In fact, I have three sitting in my kitchen right now. Several companies use this system.

STIRRER FANS IN THE CEILING, TOP FEED

A stirrer fan located in the ceiling of the microwave is another way of distributing microwave energy that comes from the top. It grabs those straight-line microwaves and throws them around, a bit like sand in a windstorm, called patterning.

You probably won't see the fan unless you stick your head in the microwave, twist your neck, and hold a flashlight in just the right spot. These machines don't guarantee perfectly even cooking, but at least any shape dish will fit.

TURNTABLES, SIDE FEED

The eternal debate continues. So many times a customer had requested a turntable. My reply was always, "Do you want a turntable, or do you want a microwave that cooks evenly?" For years people have been fed a big line that they *had* to have a turntable in order to get even cooking. As you have learned, it's just not true.

What the turntable people neglected to explain was that the microwaves, coming from the magnatron tube, only come from one opening in the microwave oven, sort of like sunlight spilling through a window onto one spot on the rug. Thus, every time your revolving food passed the magic spot, the food got a "shot" of microwave energy. The rest of the time it didn't. Yes, some stray microwaves might have been bouncing around in the microwave oven, but the result was food that was unevenly cooked. The pattern of cooking is like a bull's-eye, with the edges and the center of the food cooking first. (Remember, the center of a circle or turntable doesn't move.)

For years top-of-the-line microwaves had turntables, so people naturally associated them with quality. Today, we know better ways to distribute microwave energy.

Other practical reasons I turn you away from turntables are:

- Because turntables are round, and revolve, *many of your square or rectangle dishes won't fit inside.* So you have actually purchased a microwave about 30 percent smaller than you bargained for.
- Most turntables are glass and will break if they get too hot or you drop them. I had plenty of broken ones in my store. Cooking bagged popcorn is especially hard on them, because of the extreme heat of the popping corn. They are costly to replace.
- Turntables can be bothersome, especially if you place your container off-center. Off-center placement causes the turntable to shift and turn unevenly. And that isn't good for the microwave. What does that mean for you? You must constantly be careful to put dishes in the center of the turntable, and always distribute the food in the dishes evenly.

If you still want a turntable after all I've said, at least get one that is recessed into the floor of the microwave. It's flush and removes many of the limitations normally associated with a turntable. These microwaves have two systems: the turntable in the bottom and a stirrer fan in the ceiling. You may use the two systems separately or together, depending on the shape of your dish.

The plastic-coated turntable still can't take the heat of a

ceramic browning dish as many other microwaves can, but the recessed turntable has a useful place.

Wattage

BUT WILL IT POP POPCORN?

The amount of power or wattage, watts for short, will usually answer that important popcorn question. The number of watts is determined by the magnatron tube, which generates the high-energy waves that bombard food and get the food hot. In microwave ovens made for home use, the watts range from 300 to 800 watts.

Wattage will determine how fast your food cooks, (just like how fast your hair will dry). It's the key. The lower the wattage, the slower your food will cook. How much slower? According to *Consumer Reports* research, a 500-watt microwave is 30 percent slower than one with 700 watts. If you are reheating a cup of coffee, the time difference won't amount to much. But if you are cooking in a three-quart casserole, a lower wattage could be a difference of ten to fifteen minutes. And that could amount to a significant loss of time.

How may watts do you need? Most microwave recipes, *including the ones in this book,* have been tested in microwaves with 600 to 700 watts. This range covers the midsize and full-size microwaves.

Tiny microwaves, cute as they are, are useful for defrosting and reheating, but not much more. You will probably be happier with more wattage and more interior space than these microwaves provide.

Microwave manufacturers have come to no consensus regarding wattage standards.[2] A 600-watt microwave from

[2] According to spokesmen at IMPI, a consumer test for checking wattage is under development.

one manufacturer may differ from a 600-watt microwave by another manufacturer. And as microwaves "age," their output wattage decreases. Just as in conventional cooking, each machine is a little different. You will have to get to know your microwave. No one knows it better than you!

Some manufacturers are very liberal with their wattage claims, and others are not. And then there are the manufacturers who don't tell you the wattage at all!

If you have a burning desire to learn the approximate wattage of your machine, see Appendix A.

IT'S THE POWER, NOT THE HEAT.

HOW MANY POWER LEVELS DO YOU NEED?

Do you really need ninety-nine power levels, or will two be enough? For simplicity, relate power levels in a microwave to temperatures in a stove. The power level simply refers to the percent of time the magnatron tube is "on." Fifty percent power (medium), or just "5" on some machines, means the tube is on half the time, just as "3" or 30 percent (low) means it is on one-third of the time.

Each manufacturer has its own built-in timing cycle. Need I even *mention* that level 5 on one microwave may not be the same as power level 5 on another microwave, or that all "Mediums" are not created equally? Again, the "power" behind a power level depends on the wattage and the name the manufacturer has assigned to that power level.

The lower power levels are useful for defrosting food and low, slow simmering of tough meats and beans that will be transformed into luscious stews and soups. Just as in conventional cooking, tough foods need slow, gentle cooking to soften.

Just make sure you have at least five power levels: High (100 percent), Medium High (70 percent), Medium (50 percent), Low (30 percent), and Warm (10 percent).

Popcorn: A Billion-Dollar Industry

Microwave popcorn is a billion-dollar industry, and *you* made it happen. Americans adore popcorn, and sales of all kinds are at an all-time high.

People have actually bought a microwave oven *just to pop popcorn*. Of course, I think that is a silly way to spend a lot of money, and I used to tell my customers the same. It's all a matter of priorities, and the customer is *always right, right?*

"Scratch" microwave popcorn is a save-your-heart food and a great "fill-me-up-so-I-don't-eat-twelve-chocolate-chip-cookies food." Why do I distinguish between "scratch" and other kinds of popcorn? Calories. Fat. Sodium. Money.

If you haven't started reading labels yet, start now. Look at the calories, grams of fat, and the sodium content. All are very high. Your heart does not need this assault. Neither does your pocketbook. Microwave popcorn is expensive.

Unadorned with butter and salt, popcorn is a health snack—low in calories and fat, has no sugar or cholesterol, and is high in complex carbohydrates and dietary insoluble fiber. The American Dietetic Association, American Cancer Society, and the American Dental Association recommend popcorn.

Look at these figures for a three-cup serving:[3]

Hot Oil	Microwave Prebagged	Hot Air/Microwave Popper
11% fat	56–76% fat	5–9% fat
133 calories	145 calories	50–90 calories
1 mg sodium	236 mg sodium	1 mg sodium

[3] Figures compiled by the Popcorn Institute and nutritive analysis from Michael Jacobson, Center for Science in the Public Interest, 1875 Con-

Notice where the calories, fat, and sodium counts are highest.

I recommend an inexpensive ($10 to $15) microwave popcorn popper if you don't own an air-popper. A microwave popper fits right inside your microwave and uses regular kernels you buy in the grocery store. This method of popping corn allows you to control the amount of fat and salt yourself. Look for a popper that has a rounded or cone-shaped bottom. High heat is required for popping corn, and this V shape concentrates the heat best.

To get the best microwave "popping" results, try these tips:

1. If you are buying a microwave and want it to pop corn, ask the salesperson specifically if the model you are interested in *will* pop corn. Ask for a demonstration. Take your own microwave popcorn popper with you to the store and make sure it will fit in the microwave.

2. Wattage: Oh yes, I have heard that a minimum of six hundred watts is needed to pop popcorn. Not always true. Some 500-watt microwaves pop corn and some 650-watt ones do not. Go back to rule one: Ask the salesperson.

   Most six-hundred-watt microwaves are larger, and most poppers can only be accommodated by the larger microwaves. Tara Products (see Appendix E) makes a smaller popper.

3. *Never, never* try to pop popcorn in a paper bag. It could start a fire. Don't even *think* of doing this.

4. Don't expect every kernel in a microwave popper to pop. An 80 percent yield is about right.

5. Flavor. Some poppers give directions for add-

necticut Avene, N.W., #300, Washington, D.C. 20009. Chart from the West Bend Company, West Bend, Wisconsin.

ing oil. If you *must* have oil for flavor, add some sparingly. Of course, popcorn with no oil is a healthier snack. I like to flavor popcorn with Molly McButter or Butterbuds.

6. Wash the popper on the top shelf of the dishwasher or follow the manufacturer's instructions.

7. Don't leave home when you are popping corn! Turn the microwave off immediately when the popping slows. If you allow the corn to cook a mere ten or fifteen seconds too long, the corn will get tough and burn. Never allow popcorn to cook longer than four-and-a-half minutes.

8. Store the popcorn in the refrigerator or freezer to keep it as fresh and as full of moisture as possible.

9. Be cautious when removing the popcorn popper from the microwave—it is very hot and can burn quickly. Be especially attendant with children.

10. If you have a microwave with a glass tray or turntable, allow the glass to cool before you pop more corn. (See sad story below.)

Picture this scene.

About once a week, a frowning customer would come into my store with half of a glass tray or turntable in each hand.

ME: "Popcorn?"

HIM: "Yes."

ME: "How many batches in a row?"

HIM: "Two."

"That will be forty dollars for a new glass tray, please."

Tears began to flow as he wrote the check, and he would

mumble things like, "I told him/her *not* to do that." Then I would recommend a $9.95 microwave popcorn popper and send him to the grocery store for some inexpensive and healthy popcorn.

Another heart saved, I would think to myself.

CHAPTER 6

Features

⚬⚬⚬

The "Laundry" List

🕹 Half of the people who own microwaves are in the process of upgrading to a bigger model microwave. Microwave owners who started out with the *"never mind"* category you read about in Chapter 5, and many other people, are discovering the health benefits and convenience of microwave cooking.

Now buyers want a "real" microwave! Follow along with me and "cherry pick" your favorite features. I've listed features in the order I think are most important.

DIALS VERSUS ELECTRONIC TOUCHPADS

"WHEN I PUT IT IN THE MICROWAVE, IT WAS A MUFFIN. NOW IT'S A ROCK."
Buy a microwave with electronic controls, called a touchpad. Touchpads are easier to clean and allow greater

accuracy in selecting cooking times. Since cooking times are so much shorter in microwave cooking, seconds can mean the difference between pulling a moist muffin or a rock from the microwave.

Back in the early days, all microwaves had a dial or two (remember your old TV?) that you turned to the number of minutes you wanted to cook. You don't want that, not on a microwave, anyway. Knobs break faster, as they are spring-loaded and will eventually wear out.

PROGRAMMABILITY

All "programmability" means is that the microwave can "remember" two to four commands in sequence. All microwaves can remember one command at a time; some can remember up to four. (I wish I could say that about me.) Two or three programs are ideal. I prefer three. An example of programming is in cooking rice. This is what I "command" the microwave to do to cook 1 cup of long-grain rice:

1. Cook on High five minutes
2. Cook on Medium (50 percent) twenty minutes
3. "Stand" five minutes (you'll learn more about cooking in Chapter 8 with my Basic 101 class).

My microwave remembers the three commands and performs them in sequence without me doing anything else. At the end of the last command, the process is over. Some people call this "memory," but it is not memory as it is in a computer. For example, the microwave remembers, cooks rice, and forgets. If your microwave has programmability, find out how many commands you can give it in sequence. The answer will be from one to four.

MOISTURE SENSOR (LOVINGLY KNOWN AS THE "NO-BRAINER")

Are you the kind of person who likes to look up instructions in a book, say, at 6:00 P.M. when you walk in the house, exhausted from work? Or, on some days, do you want a machine that will do the thinking for you? If you want the easy way out, and who doesn't on certain days, choose a microwave with a moisture-sensor device. In fact, I own three of them.

Each manufacturer has its own name for this gadget with a brain. For example, "Genius," "Humidity Sensor," "Auto Cook," "Compucook," and "Aroma Sensor" all mean about the same thing.

To put the sensor feature through its paces, some manufacturers require covering the food. Newer technology does not require covering to detect moisture. (If you're not sure if you should cover or not, always refer to your Owner's Manual, as painful as that may be.)

With the push of a button, the microwave will figure out, by itself, how long the food you've shoved into it should cook. Thus, the "no-brainer."

I use the sensor a lot. I use it especially when I have an unknown quantity of food to cook or reheat, such as half of a casserole from Tuesday night's dinner, and I sure don't want to dump the contents of that half of a casserole to measure it.

The latest addition to the sensor repertoire is the popcorn sensor. Forget it. The sensor only works with prebagged microwave popcorn, which is high in sodium, fat, and calories.

Defrost Systems

For years, defrosting in the microwave has been America's favorite feature. Everybody seems to want to buy a microwave oven to defrost chicken in ten seconds flat, and cook it in another ten seconds. Defrost systems don't work quite that quickly, but the feature is a boon to anyone in a hurry. However, you've lost the excuse, "But, honey, we'll have to eat out, I forgot to take anything out of the freezer."

I rate defrost systems on a scale of *Fair, Better Yet,* and *the Winner.*

Fair is not too good. The low-end, cheapie, all-mechanical models, and some with touchpads, defrost on Low, or 30 percent power. In other words, you are defrosting on low "cook" power. Is it any surprise that your food comes out cooked on the outside before it is defrosted in the interior? Ruin a few pieces of meat or fish, and you will soon have paid for a better defrost system.

Remember, if a microwave cooks unevenly, it will defrost unevenly.

Better yet is an improvement, and usually means that a cyclical system has been used. In a cyclical system, at the beginning of defrost time, the machine is defrosting at one power level, and as the food gets more defrosted, the power levels decrease.

The Winner takes the amount of defrost time and divides the time into multiple segments, with automatic programs that pause between the times when the microwave is on.

The result of *The Winner* will be a piece of meat or other food that will be evenly defrosted without being cooked on the outside and a wad of ice on the inside. Several Japanese companies use this system.

WEIGHT DEFROST

The weight-defrost feature is *in addition* to the defrost feature that lets you defrost by time as discussed in the previous section.

Defrosting by weight is a good feature and one that works well enough. You simply "tell" the microwave how much your food (usually meat) weighs, and the microwave determines for you how long the meat should defrost. I like the feature, and use it a lot. However, I always check about midway through the defrosting time to see that my food is defrosting properly. Then I usually turn the meat over or pull the pieces apart.

Look for other variables in the food. If your food has a lot of bone, or the pieces are of uneven thickness, the result might be uneven defrosting.

TEMPERATURE PROBES

Knowing the internal temperature of your food seems like a good idea, and it is. A temperature probe looks like a metal "skewer" four to six inches long and one end is inserted into the microwave and the other into the food. It is great for meat and roast turkeys.

The probe works by computer: In some microwaves, as the probe detects the rising internal temperature of the food, the microwave automatically lowers the power level, then simply shuts the microwave off when it hits the required temperature. Others heat to the programmed temperature and cut off automatically.

I use a probe when I want to "slow cook" a stew or braise a pot roast. Surprised? Just because you usually want to cook food fast in the microwave doesn't mean that is the only way to do it. You can make a wonderful stew, cooking at low power for two or more hours. Using a probe frees you from stirring and worrying about the pan cook-

ing dry and wondering if you turned off the stove before
you left the house.

I also use a quick-read thermometer to check the internal temperature of foods.

TIMER

A timer is just what it sounds like, and is a helpful convenience to delineate standing time, or anything else you
might want to time (like teenagers on the telephone). I
use the timer constantly to remind Tex what to do next!

AUTOMATIC START/DELAY START

You'll use auto start, but not how you might think at
first. The microwave has the capability of being programmed to "turn on" as much as twelve hours ahead.
Well, nobody is going to do that—imagine sticking fish
fillets in the microwave to spend the day, unrefrigerated.

However, while you are out walking or getting dressed
or doing laundry in another part of the house, you might
want the microwave to begin cooking fifteen to thirty minutes later. That's a useful task, and one I ask my microwave to do all the time.

WEIGHT COOK

In cooking by weight, you simply program in the weight
of your food, and the microwave will determine the cooking time. Weight cook assumes your food is defrosted and
at refrigerator temperature at the start of cooking. If your
food is hotter or colder, the predetermined cooking time
might be inaccurate.

COOK CODES

Cooking by code is a feature similar to *weight cook,* but includes a wider variety of food types—such as vegetables, desserts, and convenience foods. Cook codes are particularly good for children who are learning to use the microwave and need simple instructions.

THE SHELF

Stuffing the microwave won't save you time. *A microwave cooks by volume and density—the more food you have to cook, the longer it will take.* (Don't forget this, it will be on the test at the end of the chapter!)

My feeling is that manufacturers assume we want a shelf because conventional ovens have shelves. But a shelf in a microwave works differently. If a shelf comes along with the microwave you purchase, just store it someplace. You will always cook on the bottom (the floor) of your microwave. That doesn't mean you won't use a rack or a trivet to elevate food a half-inch or so, but that is a different situation.

RECIPE MEMORY

A microwave that remembers multiple recipes for time and power is unrealistic and impractical.

THE BROWNERS:
A CATEGORY UNTO THEMSELVES

Browning systems differ in quality and effectiveness just as microwaves do.

Microwaves that brown can be divided into two types:

1. Those with some type of heating/browning element ("browners," for our purposes)

2. Those with heat and a fan (convection)

QUARTZ BROWNER

The newest browner system, the quartz browner, is usually offered on microwaves with at least 700 watts. Quartz offers much quicker browning than the radiant-heat heating element. In fact, the quartz emits a bright red glow in seconds compared to heating elements that take up to seven minutes to preheat. With a quartz browner, you won't have to wait for the browning element to preheat, leaving the microwave unavailable for use in the meantime.

Quartz is more efficient and quicker because it browns by heat *and* infrared rays. Because the quartz bulb gets very hot, wait until it cools before cleaning with a mild detergent and warm water.

Heating Elements

Remember your mama telling you that if "things" seemed too good to be true, they usually were? The same goes for microwaves with heating elements that supposedly brown. Why? First of all, the element can take as much as seven minutes to preheat. That's a long time in a microwave. Second, you cannot brown and microwave at the same time, so, while the browning element is preheating, the microwave is unavailable for cooking anything else. And the danger exists that you or your children might burn yourselves on the hot element.

If you must have a browned top on your food, put it under the broiler and use the microwave for what it does best. And if you want bread toasted, use a toaster.

MICRO/CONVECTION

CONVECTION   A lot of mystery seems to surround the micro/convection oven, but I hope it won't for long. Microconvections account for about 5 percent of all microwave sales, but sales are projected to increase to 20 percent by the end of the century. Most of these machines have part or all of the following cooking possibilities, with just the touch of a button:

- microwave
- convection
- micro/convection combination
- broiling

Convection means it's just a lot of hot air, radiant hot air that is being blown around by a fan at the back or top of the cavity. (In a conventional radiant-heat oven, the air does not move. The temperature is not always consistent, and foods usually don't brown as evenly.) Convection ovens have been used by bakeries for years. The advantage of convection is that it cooks quickly, seals in juices and moisture, and gives foods an evenly browned surface. And is a convection oven ever great for cakes and breads! The first Bundt cake I baked on the convection setting was so evenly browned, it looked as though it had been painted!

COMBINATION   And now you can get a machine that can microwave for part of the time and brown part of the time by alternating back and forth between microwave energy and convection heat. The newest microconvection version will emit microwave energy at the same time that heat is being circulated. Others automatically alternate between convection heat and microwave energy.

Why are microconvections so wonderful? Because foods cook faster because of the microwave, and brown better because of the circulating dry heat. It's the best of both worlds.

These microconvections can have all the great top-of-the-line features you would want on any microwave oven (sensor, probes, timers, etc.), so you don't have to sacrifice any features to get the convection oven too. A rotisserie, used in combination cooking, is the newest feature.

BROIL Some microconvections come with a broiling feature. Personally, if I want to broil or grill, I use my outdoor grill, or my microwave browning pan that "grills" in the microwave. Some people like the broil feature. If you choose it, prepare for extra cleaning (see Appendix E for a recommended cleaner).

If this super combo is on your "wish" list:

- Get one that is big enough to handle the foods you are likely to cook in it. A twelve- to fourteen-pound turkey, for example.
- Make sure it has at least 600 watts of microwave-energy output.
- Some of the microconvection ovens have turn-tables. One "turntable company" makes an excellent microconvection. You will have to make your own decision here.

Expect to pay more for a microwave/convection, but, don't assume that if you pay huge sums, you will get the best piece of equipment. One company I know of sells "upscale" appliances and charges a premium price for their machine. And their customers pay way too much for a machine that does not work nearly as well as some less expensive models. Make sure your prestige model delivers the quality you are paying for.

I know about these particular microconvection owners because they always found their way to my cooking classes totally lost and befuddled. Sometimes, they didn't even known how to turn on their appliance.

To date, the only microwave/convection cookbooks available are the ones that come with each individual machine. The books aren't interchangeable between brands of combination ovens.

In spite of the lack of recipe books, do I like microconvections? Yes. Are these machines perfect? No. Do I own one? Yes.

If I were designing a new kitchen, the cooking appliances I would choose would be one microwave oven, two micro/convection ovens, and a surface unit—no conventional oven. The world is not quite ready for this, but watch out, because it's coming!

MICRO/CONVECTION/BAKERY COMBINATION

This newest option will in fact make a loaf of bread. All you have to do is slip the ingredients—flour, yeast, salt, sugar, and milk—into the baking pan, maybe even the night before, and head for bed. In the morning, thanks to the preprogramming function, you will wake to the aroma of fresh hot bread.

Sound fantastic? I thought so too. But it works. Do I own one? Sorry, no. I love homemade bread *too much*. I'm still working to contain the four-hundred-pound woman inside me who is trying always to escape. Daily fresh-baked bread would give her an unfair advantage. *Just say no*, I tell myself.

Besides, $800 to $1,000 is more than I am willing to pay for a loaf of bread.

BUY AMERICAN? HOW

If you are hoping to purchase a 100 percent American-made microwave, you will have to search *real* hard. Only a couple of American companies manufacture microwaves now. In alphabetical order, they are Amana, Magic Chef, and Tappan.

However, all the models sold by a company may not be made in the same country—perhaps only a few are. For example, in addition to American-made models, Amana also had a Korean-made model or two, and Magic Chef also had some microwaves manufactured elsewhere. G.E. microwaves are manufactured by other companies. So you cannot be sure unless you ask. When all else fails, the box the microwave came in may give you a clue.

All magnatron tubes (the tube that "makes" micro-waves) and many other parts are manufactured by three Japanese companies: Hitachi, Toshiba, and Matsushita. So, even if your microwave has an American name on it, more than likely it has Japanese parts.

I am telling you this only because the country of origin might be important to you. If it is, ask your salesperson specifically *who* manufactured a particular model. Asking is the only way you will know.

REPAIRS

KEEPING THE MICROWAVE CLEAN
What or who is the biggest enemy of your magic micro-wave? You. We have met the enemy and they are *us*, as Pogo said.

- Want to stay out of the microwave repair shop?
- Want to save a $40 to $50 service call?
- Want years of happy microwaving?

It's simple.
Keep the microwave clean.

I was truly astounded at some of the dirty microwaves that came to our repair shop, since the owners usually looked clean and nicely put together. I won't even tell you what you would find if you were to take the outside covering off the microwave. (Please don't try it.) If your microwave is being abused with spilled food and grease, inside and out, *shame on you.*

Let me say it one more time: Keep it clean. And do not use cleaners with ammonia, as it will "cloud" the plastic. (See Appendix E.)

You see, a microwave does not discriminate. The waves will cook anything in sight. Grease buildup will decrease efficiency and increase chance for arcing (sparking a fire), thus increasing your chances for a trip to the repair shop. Spend your money on something else.

Of course, the machine can fail through no fault of your own. Call that manufacturer failure, not your failure. You are an innocent victim here. If this happens, go back to the store where you bought the microwave and get advice on how to proceed with the company. See Appendix E for manufacturer telephone numbers and other information on where to find help.

YES, MADAM, THE PATIENT WILL LIVE

Microwave owners would cry if we couldn't treat the broken "patient" on an immediate outpatient basis. Sometimes these owners needed "therapy." Heaven forbid if a part had to be ordered and people had to use other means to cook their food. Anyone who owns a microwave understands. I understand. I cried when I had *only one* microwave.

WARRANTIES

About warranties: In general, microwave warranties are good for one year for parts and labor, five years (parts only) for the magnatron tube. Of course, warranties vary from company to company. Read the fine print and save your sales invoice.

The Machine

More "old wives' tales" probably exist about microwaves than any other kitchen tool. The government now has stringent design specifications to insure safety. Worries about radiation leakage are far behind us. Better design, tighter, heavy plastic doors, and stronger safety standards have removed those risks.

SAFETY TIPS

When cooking in the microwave, use the same common sense you would use with any hot food: use hot pads, open lids and coverings away from your face, don't leave utensils that might absorb heat in your food while it is cooking, and use microwave-safe dishes for cooking.

If you cook a food with a high-sugar "center"—like a jelly doughnut, heaven forbid—be very careful, because the higher-sugar content in the center will be *hot* compared to the outside. Children and the elderly need to be cautioned of this difference.

Don't heat baby bottles in the microwave, as the milk may get too hot and burn the baby's mouth. Be extra cautious if you heat *any* of baby's food in the microwave.

Undercooked food could be a hazard. Because foods stay in the microwave for such a short amount of time, some foods such as chicken, pork, and fish are vulnerable to undercooking. The cooking time might not be sufficient to kill harmful microbes. Chicken, pork, and fish require sufficient cooking time. Be cautious. Check Appendix D for the correct internal temperatures of many foods.

For safety's sake, use a microwave that cooks evenly, or else rotate the food during cooking to prevent "cold spots," which are really "undercooked" spots. You should check the internal temperature of certain foods, especially meats, in several places.

Standing time is crucial. Allow most foods (exceptions will be noted in the recipe) to "stand" covered, after cooking. Then, the heat that has concentrated in the exterior edges of the food has a chance to radiate to the center to cook the food and equalize the temperature throughout.

Some food scientists worry that plastic wraps may melt onto the cooking food. I use glass covers (and containers) whenever possible. When it's not practical or possible to use a lid, I usually use a brand of plastic wrap called Stretch Tite* (see Appendix E), or Glad Cling Wrap.† No matter what brand I use, I *do not* let the plastic wrap come in contact with the food. I allow plenty of headroom (at least one inch) space for "boil-ups." I cover *dishes*, not *food*, with the wrap.

Always defrost foods before starting to cook them. If you don't defrost first, the food could cook unevenly.

*Mail order
†Available in grocery stores

I hope this information on feature-mania has helped clear the microwave waters. Take this book with you when you go shopping. No one can remember all of the necessary details.

And now, on to pots and pans.

CHAPTER 7

Accessories to Make Your Cooking Easier

🕉🕉🕉

🕉 Do I have to buy all new cookware just to save my heart with the microwave? Of course not. All new cookware isn't *essential*, but some microwave-designed accessories will make your life easier. Not buying good cookware is a bit like owning the best set of golf clubs but having no good balls to play with.

Naturally, I have save-your-heart accessory recommendations for you. The list is personal, and includes accessories I find most useful for healthy microwave cooking.

Ya Gotta Have Its

BATTER BOWLS/MEASURING CUPS One of the best cooking utensils you may already have is an assortment of microwave-safe glass measuring cups. I use them for most of my chores—the small ones for melting margarine and cooking and reheating small amounts of food, to the large ones, called batter bowls, for cooking vegetables and puddings, simmering soups, cooking rice, and, yes, for mixing batters, to name just a few examples.

Make sure you buy *batter bowls* with handles attached at the top only, and open at the bottom (open handles will absorb less heat and be cooler to touch). Convenient sizes to own are 8, 16, 32, 48, and 64 ounces (1, 2, 4, 6, and 8 cups). I refer to batter bowls constantly in recipes when I say, "in a 4- to 6-cup measure."

You'll be amazed how often you will use measure/cook containers. In fact, you'll get spoiled.

BROWNING GRILL   This browning accessory is to a microwave as a skillet is to a stove. Of course, it doesn't "fry" in the conventional sense but does give foods a crisper and browned surface, just as does your outdoor grill or conventional broiler.

The flat browning *grill* will accommodate several fillets of fish or pieces of chicken. I use the grill constantly for fish—I especially like salmon and tuna steaks cooked this way. You will also like the way the grill works with other fish, chicken, and grilled sandwiches, even French Toast.

The browning accessory needs to be preheated. The instructions that accompany it will give you the details of how long to preheat for each particular food you intend to cook. You will want to refer to your owner's manual also to make sure the browning accessory is approved to use in your microwave.

Some of these grills can go in the dishwasher and some cannot. This is one accessory I would own whether it was dishwasher-safe or not.

A SAFETY NOTE:

Always use hot pads while handling a browning accessory, and caution children who may discover its usefulness for cooking *pizza*!

COLANDER   Colanders go by lots of names in the microwave world—ground-meat cooker, strainer, Cook 'n Drainer, or *colander*. I'll call it a colander here and throughout the recipes in this book. It is indispensable to the recipes in *Save Your Heart with Susan*. By allowing meat fats to drain away as the meat cooks, a colander lowers the fat (and calorie) level of so many dishes. And since animal fat is a main culprit in heart disease and other diseases, getting the fat out and keeping the flavor in are our main goals.

Most microwave specialty stores carry a colander or meat cooker/drainer, and sometimes it will come as part of a cookware set. If you use a plastic colander that did not come with a set, be sure it is microwave-safe. Rubbermaid and Tara Products are two companies that manufacture products that can be used to drain away fats and liquid to save your heart. A microwave specialty store may have other brands (see Appendix E).

FOOD SCALE   The microwave oven cooks by weight and volume, and many jobs, from defrosting to steaming, are calculated in minutes per pound. Choose a *scale* that measures ounces and pounds. A scale doesn't have to be expensive, and it will become one of your most-used kitchen accessories. I couldn't get along without a kitchen scale.

MUFFIN PAN   This is a round baking dish with six or seven cups for muffins. A *muffin pan* promotes even cooking of muffins, steamed eggs, even miniature meat loaves. The cups in the pan make it convenient to reheat "dabs" of leftovers. Each cup doesn't have to be filled in order to use the pan. Tara Products makes a muffin pan safe for the microwave and up to 450 degrees in a conventional oven. (Individual custard cups can be substituted for a muffin pan.)

THERMOMETER   Temperature taking is a useful task employed by almost everybody, including microwave cooks. Check the temperature of the food you are:

1. taking out of the microwave
2. reheating, for safety's sake

For those times when you need a *thermometer* (and can't find the temperature probe that came with your microwave), Taylor makes an excellent one to be used in the microwave oven. The thermometer is instant read, which requires you to wait only a few seconds to learn the temperature of your food. Because the thermometer is designed for microwave use, you can actually leave it in the food, inside the microwave. (Don't try this with thermometers that aren't made exclusively for microwave use; the mercury will separate.)

Using a thermometer regularly, especially until you get the hang of cooking times and standing times, will prevent dried out and overcooked food (chicken) or raw, hard, or undercooked (vegetables) food. See Appendix D for a guide to temperatures.

TRIVET   A *trivet* elevates the food and allows air to circulate around the items so that moisture does not collect in the bottom and cause a soggy potato or roll. You will also use it when you are cooking vegetables and sometimes poultry. Tara Products makes an inexpensive one (see Appendix E).

UTILITY RACK   Back in the "bad ole days" we called this accessory a bacon rack. But since we *rarely if ever eat bacon anymore*, we've changed the name. The *utility rack* is a "must have" as basic cookware. You will use it to defrost, sometimes to reheat, and often to cook foods like meat or turkey loaf, chicken, turkey, and fish. So buy the biggest size you can find that will fit in your microwave. Make sure the rack has enough "trough" around the edges to collect grease and moisture and is easy to clean.

Utility racks (as well as other microwave plastics) do stain, so be prepared for that (see **TIP** for cleaning, page 190). And also make sure the one you buy is dishwasher-safe.

VARIOUS BAKING DISHES As you start cooking regularly in the microwave, you will bless the day you received your first Pyrex baking dishes. An assortment of different sizes is essential. You will use them, and dishes like them, constantly. Daily. Hourly. No metal trim, please.

You Might Already Have Its

Some items are so basic, and so important, that I assume you will always keep them around the house.

You will use *plastic wrap* as a covering or when a lid is not practical or available. See p. 98.

Aluminum foil will come in handy to cover the edges of a casserole or the tips of chicken wings, or to slow the cooking of part of a dish for even cooking (see Chapter 8 for information on shielding).

Paper towels absorb moisture and make wonderful "lids" for heating sandwiches, and for soaking grease under meats and moisture from potatoes. To be microwave-safe, always use white paper towels, and never use any paper products made with recycled paper. Recycled products often contain tiny metal flecks that will cause arcing (sparking) and possible damage to the microwave. When I refer to "microwave paper towels" in my recipes, I am talking about towels *not* made with recycled paper. Bounty Microwave Towels are my favorite brand.

For safety's sake, don't use paper towels as plates; they aren't sturdy enough. Paper products for cooking, such as paper towels, napkins, cups, and plates, including Styrofoam, are commonly used in microwave ovens. And they commonly cause burning accidents when they fold, spill, and split apart. I don't use paper products for cooking myself, and don't recommend that others use them either. They're just too dangerous. I am ultraconservative when it comes to your safety and mine.

Wax paper makes a good "lid" when you want to control spatters and still allow some moisture to escape.

DON'T FORGET TO STIR!

Wooden spoons and regular rubber *spatulas* are useful, and I especially like spoon/spatulas made by Rubbermaid. Metal spoons and tongs can be used to stir or turn food. Just don't plan to leave anything metal in the pan during cooking, as the heat from the food will be conducted to the utensil and can cause a burn. I did it only once, and I was sorry.

Some wooden spoons can get hot in the microwave if you wash them in the dishwasher. In the dishwasher, some of the protective coating may wash off. Then, during cooking, the wood will absorb water. The water in the spoon will heat in the microwave and make the spoon hot.

SAFETY FIRST

Hot pads: You only have to get burned once to know that pans will get hot in the microwave oven. Keep the mitts close and use them. As foods cook, they become hot, and the heat is transferred to the container. Be sure to caution children.

GO ON A TREASURE HUNT
FOR BASIC KITCHEN GEAR

You may find many hard plastic bowls, plates, and containers hiding in a forgotten corner. Look for the words "microwave safe" on the underside, as they have been tested to withstand microwave food-cooking temperatures. After you do the cookware test that I describe below, you may be able to use your own dishes. You may use wood and straw containers for *quickly* heating rolls; just don't plan to bake a casserole in them.

Of course, you have to avoid any metal pans or dishes not especially designed for the microwave. Metal reflects the microwaves and can cause sparks, called arcing, which will damage the microwave oven.

Be sure to avoid soft plastics, such as margarine, cottage-cheese, or any similar containers. These containers are meant for storage of food and cannot withstand microwave cooking temperatures. They, like plastic wraps, can melt on or in your food. Be sure to caution children.

Don't use dishes or cups, like your "good" china, that may have bands of silver or other metal on them—they react by arcing as described above.

TESTING . . . TESTING YOUR DISHES FOR MICROWAVE SAFETY

Use this simple test to determine if your dish will work in the microwave oven.

1. Fill a 1-cup glass measure with water and set it in the microwave oven.
2. Set an empty container, such as a coffee cup or casserole dish, next to the cup of water.
3. Microwave on High for one to two minutes.
4. If the water is warm and the empty container is cool after the allotted cooking time, the container is suitable for microwaving. But if the water is cool and the container is warm or hot in spots, it is not suitable. The container has absorbed microwave energy instead of letting it pass through. If you were to use this container, the dish would cook and your food would not.

You Decide If You Need Its

What is a necessity for you may be a luxury for me. You might not be able to live without a popcorn popper. I rarely eat popcorn. It's personal. The items on the following list fall into that personal category—you may find them useful, even indispensable. I'm offering my opinions on them, and they are listed in no particular order.

MICROWAVE COOKWARE SETS Several companies sell sets of bowls and pans in various sizes. The sets are useful, and, frankly, I don't know how I would get along without the sets I own. In addition to the basic pans, most sets include a variety of items, from popcorn poppers and racks to colanders and storage lids. Sets are an economical way to get a wide variety of cookware that you might not purchase individually. Some plastics can even withstand up to 450 degrees.

CLAY COOKWARE The beautiful clay baking pot works wonderfully well in the microwave. Its success lies in the way it seals in flavor and moisture, penetrating and blending with the natural food juices to increase tenderness.

One of the best-known brands of clay cookware is the Romertopf. Of course, you will want to soak it each time before using, as soaking is the secret to the moist food that clay cookware produces, and follow the manufacturer's directions. The clay baker also comes with a recipe booklet, so just apply your Save Your Heart with Susan principles to the recipes. The bakers come in various sizes. The embossed terra-cotta clay goes easily from microwave to the table, with no apologies from you. Whatever brand of claybaker you choose, make sure it is microwave-safe.

For general directions, presoak the baker, then start cooking on High power, and later, reduce power to Medium (50 percent) for the remainder of the cooking time.

Of course, you will let the food "stand" for a few minutes, as you do with all foods cooked in the microwave. The best foods for the clay baker are meats, poultry, and dried beans.

The main point I caution you about is that clay bakers break easily, so "handle with care." I know—I've lost several. I keep replacing them because I like the way they cook so much—so easy and so delicious.

POPCORN POPPER   I have actually known people to buy a microwave oven just so they could cook popcorn. While I don't condone such foolishness, microwave popcorn is convenient. Popcorn cooks fast, with no mess, oil, or fuss, and it is a healthy snack. Popcorn can easily fit into your plan to save your heart. (Not the prebagged kind; see Popcorn, page 80.)

With the microwave popcorn popper, you can use "regular" popping corn. Be sure to choose a microwave popper that has a rounded or V-shaped bottom for the popcorn, rather than a doughnut-shaped indention. The V shape will concentrate the microwave energy to give you better results.

PORTABLE TURNTABLES   By now you should have an idea of what I think of turntables as part of the microwave. If you buy a microwave oven with good microwave energy distribution to begin with, the turntable is unnecessary.

However, if you have an old microwave oven and you know it has hot spots, a portable turntable might have a place. Just make sure your dishes and cookware still fit in the microwave with the turntable in place. Turntables take up to two or more inches of height in your microwave, have weight limitations, are "spring-loaded," and have to be rewound in order to turn.

Most turntables sound as if a wild animal is trying to escape from your microwave, so check its noise level before you buy.

PRESSURE COOKER This "cooker" combines microwave speed with old-fashioned pressure cooking for moist and tender meats and stews. Some people swear by them. Because the cooker draws moisture to the food rather than away from it, meat will not dry out. And it reduces microwave cooking time up to 35 percent.

The pressure cookers do have some requirements. You will need a microwave oven with at least six hundred watts, and nine inches interior headroom.

Many customers liked this product. Personally, I don't like to have to "brown" food on top of the stove before I cook it. Maybe you don't mind. They cost between $25 and $35, so read the fine print before you plunge.

ROASTER Even if you're a diehard microwave cooker, once in a while you're going to want to make a "roast." It's the American way, after all. But, by definition, "roast" means dry heat. And, because the microwave uses a moist cooking method, it *cannot roast.*

With the Magna Wave roaster, you *can* roast in the microwave.

"Sure," I said. You see, I'm very suspicious of many new microwave gadgets. Some of them are fine; however, a lot of them are useless gadgets seemingly dreamed up in an undergraduate marketing class.

The Magna Wave machine I liked. (The roaster comes with specific instructions that you *must* read.) It's a metal roaster with an aluminum rack that sits, elevated on ridges, at the bottom of the container. The rack keeps food above the liquid in the bottom of the pan. The metal keeps the liquid from heating and turning to steam (remember micro *waves* cannot penetrate metal), and therefore *dry* heat is produced, not moist heat. The lid is tempered glass, and what you get is browned meat, not gray meat. What a change!

The roaster comes in two sizes with a small recipe book.

(Under torture, I admitted the Magna Wave roaster is safe to use in a conventional oven.)

OTHER MISCELLANEOUS ITEMS Potato bakers (I never use), splatter screens (I never use), Bundt pans with a hole in the middle (indispensable at my house), and an egg cooker (I use twice a year and love it) vegetable steamer/pasta cooker (makes excellent pasta), and a microwave coffeepot (I never use). See what I mean about personal? I use some of these occasionally, couldn't live without others.

CHAPTER 8

Basic Microwave Cooking 101, or "See Spot Run"

ಞಞಞ

Opening the Box

☎ You've bought the newest version of the contraption everyone has been talking about, perhaps even taken it out of the packaging. This metal "box" of a microwave is sitting on your kitchen counter. Booklets and warranties and instructions are spilling out around you.

And now "buyer's remorse" sets in. You're thinking, "Oh, why did I buy this big a machine? It takes up too much counter space, and I shouldn't have spent so much money, and now I have to relearn everything about cooking and, and, and . . ."

Hold the phone! Everything is going to be okay. You are going to love your new microwave, but just not this minute. Think of a food you didn't like the first time you tasted it. Oysters, or Mexican food, perhaps. You kept trying to eat oysters, and eventually you adored them. Cooking in the microwave will be the same.

Or, you likely could be one of the eight out of ten

American microwave owners who love to use your microwave to reheat and defrost. (If I had a nickel—make that a dollar—for every time a customer said *that* to me, I wouldn't be writing this book; I would be in rich people's paradise, wherever that is.) But I'm talking about *Using your machine for something else—like cooking . . . to . . . save your heart!*

Even though you may have owned a microwave for several years or more and know some of its features, I want you to explore your microwave *as if you just unpacked the box*. And even if you say, "I use my microwave every day," I won't be impressed until you say "I *cook* in my microwave every day."

I'm going to make learning to *cook* in your microwave as painless for you as possible and take you right through the paces as fast as I can—all you have to do is follow along, and you will have your own personalized cooking class. I would be there with you if I could be, as I was for thousands of other beginning microwave cooks.

COMMON SENSE COMES IN HANDY

First, a word about common sense. Using yours goes a long way toward becoming a good microwave cook, just as it does for other kinds of cooking. If you are a *good* "other" kind of cook, *you will be a good microwave cook.* And if you are a *bad* cook, you will be a *fast bad cook* using the microwave.

Using what you already know makes so much sense. Just because you are cooking in a different machine doesn't mean you have to throw out every bit of knowledge you already have about cooking in general. Many of the same principles apply. You'll see that as you read on.

Let's get started. Remember to keep an open mind throughout the whole learning process. Learning to use your microwave will be a bit like learning to read "See Spot Run," of Dick, Jane, and Sally fame.

WHEN ALL ELSE FAILS,
READ THE INSTRUCTIONS . . . THREE TIMES.

You won't like the first item I'm going to tell you, but do it anyway. Read the Owner's Manual or the Use and Care Manual that came with your microwave. Just realize that you won't understand the information the first or even the second time you read it. On the third try, take the manual and a measuring cup of water and go stand in front of your microwave. Go ahead. You guessed it—the water goes inside. We want the microwave energy to have something to "work on," and a cup of water is an easy, inexpensive target. Even though *Save Your Heart with Susan* is a basic book, the Owner's Manual will tell you about the features of *your* microwave.

The people who write Owners' Manuals are not really sadistic people, they just don't know how to write technical information in a simple manner. Just do what they tell you to do, as best you can, and accept the fact that most manufacturers' manuals are *not* "user friendly." I have noticed that once you know how to work your microwave, the directions in the operations manual will become crystal clear! I can't explain it. It's just true.

Some Basic Terms, Techniques, and Explanations

Not all foods cook the same way or at the same speed. The following list of terms and techniques will explain a few of the variables.

RANGE OF COOKING TIMES

Get ready for an important rule, and imprint it on your brain.

Do not overcook.

Write that sentence five hundred times please! Keep your pen handy for another rule!

You can always add cooking time. Once a muffin is a rock, it's a rock forever.

For this reason, plus the many variables that add quirks to any method of cooking, most microwave cooking times are given in ranges, e.g., one to three minutes or fifteen to twenty-five seconds. Always choose the shortest cooking time in the range and add time if it is needed. And remember that "standing" time (see below) contributes to the "doneness" of a dish.

If, after standing, the food is still not cooked to your satisfaction, put it back into the microwave and add a little more time. One last word: Don't overdo it. The last half of the cooking time needs your attention the most— that's when the heat has accumulated in your food, and it is cooking *faster*. Common sense will go a long way.

STANDING (RESTING, CARRY-OVER COOKING) TIME

These terms all mean the same thing. Microwaves penetrate three-quarter to one-and-a-half inches into your food. In order to cook food through to the center, heat must be conducted there. *Standing (resting)* time allows enough time for those gyrating molecules that produce heat to travel to the center of the food.

The same conduction occurs during defrosting, when standing time allows ice crystals time to warm enough to thaw the food and equalize the temperature throughout the food. When the microwave is turned off, the "waves" are off. However, the heat that has been generated by the "waves" continues to penetrate and conduct heat. Conduction helps give even cooking *and* even defrosting.

THESE ALSO AFFECT COOKING TIMES

VOLUME AND DENSITY

Microwaves cook by *volume* and *density*—the more food you put in a microwave, the longer the food takes to cook. Ten pounds of potatoes would cook faster in a conventional oven. Also, some foods (carrots, for example) are very dense. Other foods are not dense, such as an airy croissant. The carrot will take longer to cook because it is more dense. The croissant will take less time because it is porous. Simple, eh? Read on.

What is density, really? Density is how many molecules occupy a certain amount of space. The more molecules in a space, the denser the food, and the longer it takes for the heat to penetrate. Now you can see the problem of trying to cook meat (dense), potatoes (dense), and bread (porous) together in the microwave at the same time. The bread would overcook long before the roast was done.

Because foods have different densities, you will have better results if you cook them separately. Cook the meat first, if it is a roast, followed by the potato, and finish with the bread. Call it sequential cooking, one thing right after another.

Bones also alter the cooking times for meat. The bone acts as a "conductor" of heat, a bit like electricity running through a wire. The meat nearest the bone will cook faster.

WATER (OR MOISTURE), FAT, SUGAR

Foods with higher *moisture* content cook faster than foods low in moisture. Fish, sauces, tomatoes, onions, and many vegetables are high in moisture and cook quickly. But dried peas, beans, and rice have very little moisture and need more cooking time to be rehydrated.

Popcorn has essentially no moisture, as you learned in the popcorn section. The microwaves have to work *hard* to "pop" corn.

Another favorite target of microwave energy is *fat*. Microwaves like fat almost as much as Americans do. you will see *how much* microwaves like fat when you cook bacon later—not to eat, but to observe browning and *grease*.

Sugar is another favorite of microwaves. The "waves" go straight to high concentration of sugar and heat them quickly.

SIZE AND SHAPE OF FOOD
- The *size* of food affects cooking time. Foods cut in two- to three-inch pieces seem to cook best. No, I don't mean that you have to cut everything in two-inch pieces; I'm giving you the ideal. You have to balance the ideal with the practical! Common sense!
- The *shape* of food is important in another way— the microwave cooks foods more evenly when the foods are in a round container. Shape is the reason instructions for baking potatoes call for placing the potatoes in a "spoke" fashion. Cakes, and even meat loaves, are frequently baked in a round dish, often with a hole in the middle for more even cooking.

STARTING TEMPERATURE OF FOOD
The *starting temperature* of food also affects cooking time. Cold food takes longer to cook than room-temperature food. You already knew that, I bet. You used your common sense. Save it, you'll need it again later!

MORE TERMS

This list of cooking terms and explanations is one you will see throughout the recipes in this and most other microwave cookbooks.

COVERING

Covering foods with the correct cover will bring better cooking results. Learning the difference between the various types of coverings and how they will affect your recipes and cooking is *very important*. A few simple rules will speed your success.

Use *lids and plastic wrap* (see page 98 for precautions) to hold in moisture and distribute heat more evenly.

White microwave paper towels absorb moisture (reheating and defrosting dinner rolls, reheating sandwiches). See page 103.

Any brand of *wax paper* is okay.

Aluminum foil—yes, friends, aluminum foil. Now just listen to me before you panic. You'll use foil to "shield" (see below) or to force microwave energy to enter your food at a different location.

REARRANGING

This means to move one piece of food from one location on the dish to another location. Why, you say? You probably remember that microwaves penetrate about one inch, and then food cooks by heat conduction. *Rearranging* will allow more even cooking on all sides of the food. Foods that can't be stirred are usually rearranged for more even cooking. Chicken pieces often need to be moved around, for example.

STIRRING

Many foods need to be stirred whether they are cooked by microwaves or conventional methods. By *stirring,* you are moving the food from the edge of the dish, where the food is hotter, and mixing it with the cooler food in the center to equalize the temperature.

The rule is, you stir when you can, and you rearrange when you can't.

SHIELDING

You should be familiar with *shielding* already, as you probably use it in conventional cooking. Shielding is just as crucial in microwave recipes to slow down cooking in certain areas of a dish. Aluminum foil is most commonly used to shield, because *microwaves cannot pass through metal.* Shielding is helpful to:

- keep foods from being overcooked
- prevent overcooked corners when using a square pan
- prevent overcooking of "thin-skinned" areas like turkey wings

VENTING

Coverings such as plastic wrap should be vented. The term *venting* means to fold back a corner of the plastic wrap to let some steam escape. Some microwave experts do not recommend venting. I do; I think it's safer. I've seen too many burns (some were my own) from a bubble of hot steam trying to escape from a cooking dish. Venting also prevents the plastic from being "sucked down" on the food and creating a vacuum.

Tests and More Tests

TEST FOR HOT SPOTS

The very first microwave cooking mystery to solve is to get to know *your* microwave. No one will know it as *you do.* Just as you already know your conventional oven and its "hot spots," you will want to know the idiosyncrasies of your microwave.

Does your microwave have any hot spots, and where are those nasty places? Most microwaves will have one or two, and the same goes for cold spots. If you know where they are in your machine, you can cook accordingly and get better results. A simple test will check the cooking pattern of your microwave. Do this test now and save yourself grief later. The test won't take long.

1. Cover the bottom of your microwave with regular-thickness white bread, with crusts touching.
2. Cook on High 4 to 7 minutes *or* until you begin to see browning of the bread. The toasted or browned areas will show where the concentrations of microwave energy are located.
3. Now that you know where these tricky spots are, you can place or turn your food for more even cooking.

If your microwave has a number of hot spots, you may want to purchase a turntable, as discussed in Chapter 4. *The recipes in this book do not tell you to turn your food during the cooking process, because my microwaves cook very evenly. Yours may not.*

I'll say this now: *If your microwave cooks unevenly, turn your food as often as it needs it!*

Now, the long-awaited recipe . . . ta-da:

HOW TO BOIL WATER

Now I know you are thinking, "Susan Nicholson, you are insulting me." Not true. I'm doing this because I love you, not because I want to torture you. You'll be glad, I promise.

You see, I'm really saving you from ruining food. Water is inexpensive (so far). You also won't be frustrated with failure. Stress won't help *save your heart* either.

Fill one microwave-safe measuring cup with eight ounces of water. Microwave on High for three to four minutes or until boiling.

There, you did it! You can now have some herb tea to soothe your nerves, and enjoy your second microwave accomplishment. Cooking in the microwave is going to get lots better. This is all for today. Making out your grocery list for your practice cooking lessons is all that is left of today's lesson. Better yet, I'll make it out for you. After you have read through *all* the lessons, buy the food and paper products on the list. Don't ask why—yet.

Grocery List

Food

Potato:	1 6- to 8-ounce of the baking type, the roundest one you can find (and it won't be easy)
Corn:	1 ear, fresh or frozen
Broccoli:	1 cup, fresh
Carrots:	2 fresh
Chicken:	1 breast half and 1 leg
Vegetable-oil margarine:	2 teaspoons
Lean ground beef:	8 ounces
Paprika:	a few shakes

Marshmallows:	2 large
Some kind of roll or bun	1 each
Bacon:	4 slices. Don't be alarmed! This bacon is not for you to eat, but to teach you how fats cook in the microwave.

Paper products

Microwave paper towels
Wax paper
Aluminum foil
Plastic wrap

Equipment you will need

Shallow baking dish or pie pan
1 one-cup measuring cup, microwave-safe
1 two-cup measuring cup or bowl, microwave-safe
Scissors
Pastry brush
Custard cup

See you in your kitchen . . . for some real *cooking* with your microwave.

CHAPTER 9

Basic Microwave Cooking 102: The Lessons

ॐॐॐ

Just "A Few Good Men," Please

❷ I have learned that formal education has little to do with successful microwave cooking. Successful cooks have four characteristics:

- Desire
- Determination
- Common Sense
- A Sense of Humor

The Rayfields exhibited all four characteristics. This is their story.

Mr. and Mrs. Rayfield came to see me in my microwave store after they had seen me on TV several times. They wanted to learn how to *cook* in a microwave oven, and purchased a good one (their first) and appropriate cookware. They both came to cooking classes (30 percent of my students were men; for some reason more men attend microwave cooking classes than "other" kinds of cooking classes). Did buying a good microwave, appropriate cookware, and coming to class turn them into great microwave cooks? It helped, of course, but no, their determination and sense of humor made the difference.

Each week they would tell me the foods they had cooked (usually the same ones I had cooked in class) and their results—some good, some not so good. In other words, they practiced.

I remember one day distinctly. Mrs. Rayfield charged into the store on a day other than class day. While gritting her teeth, she said, "Susan, I am determined to get those muffins right. I saw you do them on TV, and *I know I can do it*. I tried last night, and they were like rocks." Then she opened her purse and handed me two of these "rocks." (I think she had heard about my "rock collection" from other students.) "But I'm going to *get them right*." She laughed at herself, then rushed out of the store.

I know she will be a successful microwave cook because she has *the* important characteristics.

By the way, the Rayfields are in their seventies.

That event made my day. People like the Rayfields make *me* do my recipes over and over until I *get them right*. I dedicate Basic 101 and 102 to the Rayfields, and people like them everywhere.

The Plan

You are going to learn to cook in the microwave in six *easy* lessons. Write these sentences down before you begin.

- I want to learn to *cook* in my microwave.
- I will *practice* until I get it right.
- I will *use* what I already know about cooking and will *learn* new microwave techniques.

- I will *laugh* at myself and torture anyone else who makes fun of my less-than-successful first microwave-cooking efforts.

Sign your name and paste this pledge near your microwave, on the bathroom mirror, and at any other important communication centers in your house. Put the family on notice that you are learning to cook in the microwave.

Every day, you will prepare a minimum of one and a maximum of three foods from the foods you just purchased. (If you are doing just one item a day, buy your meat and chicken closer to the days when you can practice.)

Notice, I said *practice*. This is not food to serve your family. You can taste this food, but do not prepare it with dinner in mind. Go through the exercises immediately after finishing a meal or on your days off, if you have such a thing. If at all possible, allow yourself fifteen minutes practice time for each session.

When you get home from the marathon shopping spree, treat yourself to another cup of the herb tea you learned to prepare in the last chapter.

The Lessons

You will be more successful if you read through the complete lesson before you begin.

LESSON 1: POTATOES

In this lesson, you will learn:

- to cook a potato
- to pierce to release steam

- the use of standing time
- placement for even cooking

You will need:

- 1 potato
- fork
- paper towels
- aluminum foil

And now on to some great microwave cooking results: your first *really good* baked potato. (The perfect potato requires a trivet.)

The potato should weigh 6 to 8 ounces, and it should be as round as possible to insure *even cooking*. Scrub the potato with a brush and *pierce* it twice with a fork to vent. Piercing breaks open the skin so that it won't explode all over the microwave. (Now, if you've had a particularly bad day, just keep piercing. It won't hurt the potato, and it may help get out your aggressions and save your heart.)

Place the potato on a paper towel and cook it on High 7 to 9 minutes *per pound*, or 4 to 4½ minutes per potato. When you take the potato out of the microwave, it will still be almost hard. Resist the temptation to put it back in and cook it more. Instead, wrap the potato in a fresh paper towel, then wrap it in aluminum foil and let the potato "stand" or rest for five more minutes.

For a review of *standing time,* refer to page 113 in Chapter 8. Standing time is an important part of cooking in the microwave, so just plan to include standing time in your meal-preparation time. (Potatoes are dense, so you would prepare them before other more porous foods and let them "stand" while you prepare the rest of the meal. Potatoes will stay hot for 30 to 40 minutes wrapped in foil.

You may wonder if you need to leave the potato in the microwave or take it out during standing time. Where you put it doesn't matter to the potato, but you might want to use your microwave for other cooking; so I'd just take the potato out of the microwave and put it on the counter. If you cook more than one potato, wrap them in a paper-towel "bundle" and then in a terry-cloth towel "bundle."

Resist the temptation to ignore standing time in recipes. Using standing time as recommended will mean the difference between success and failure.

After the standing time, remove the foil and paper towel. Notice that the towel is damp and the skin of the potato is dry. If you had *not* used the towel, you would now have a soggy-skinned potato.

Remember your principle on volume and density? Apply it here. If you cook baked potatoes for the family, just remember, baking two potatoes takes longer than baking one. And placement is crucial for even cooking when you have more than one potato. Always arrange the potatoes in a *circle or spoke fashion* when you have more than one or two.

LESSON 2: OTHER VEGETABLES

In this lesson, you will learn:

- to cook corn on the cob, broccoli, and carrots
- to vent and why
- when to add salt

You will need:

- corn on the cob
- broccoli
- carrots
- plastic wrap
- paring knife

- scissors
- microwave-safe dish or two-cup measure

I chose corn, broccoli, and carrots because you will learn different techniques with each. Begin with the corn.

CORN   Use your scissors and cut off the silk that is hanging out the end of the ear and break off the long stalk if necessary. Now, if you don't like mystery and you just can't deal with the fact that an itsy-bitsy worm could be hiding in there, peel back the husk a bit and check. Then wrap the ear, husk and all, in microwave-safe plastic wrap.

If you spot "fresh" corn on the cob that looks as though it might be a week past its prime, you can use it anyway. Just soak the ears in their husks in a sink of water for about 15 minutes before cooking. Soaking will "inject" some moisture and make the corn cook and taste as if it were fresh.

(Note: If corn in the husk is not available, purchase frozen corn on the cob. Wrap the corn in *wax* paper or put the corn in a deep glass baking dish, add a tablespoon of water, and cover the dish with plastic wrap.)

Put the corn in the microwave and cook on High for 3 minutes (2 minutes if you have a fresh ear with no husk). Then let it *stand* for 3 to 5 minutes. Make a cut in the plastic with your scissors, down the length of the ear, and peel back the husk. The corn will be *hot,* so use *hot pads,* and direct the steam away from you. The silk will literally "melt away" as you pull down the husk.

You have just prepared the best ear of corn you will have ever tasted. In the future, if you cook more than one ear at a time, place them in the microwave spoke fashion for even cooking.

BROCCOLI   Wash and put about 1 cup of fresh florets in a microwave-safe dish or 2-cup measure. Cover it with plastic wrap and just fold back a corner of the plastic to vent (see page 117). You don't need to add any water other than that which clings to the broccoli from washing. Cook on High for about 1 minute. Test the broccoli with a fork to see if it is hot all the way through. Then let it *stand* one or two minutes, covered.

LEARN TO LOVE CRUNCH Cooking vegetables for short periods of time to keep them crunchy goes *against every rule* I learned as a child. No self-respecting vegetable in our house was ever cooked to be crunchy. We cooked green beans for days before we declared them edible. I'm telling you this because I have had to *learn* to like crunchy vegetables instead of 8:00 P.M. cafeteria vegetables. If I can do it, so can you!

Healthy vegetables should be crunchy. You probably noticed that we haven't added any seasoning to our vegetables. In microwave cooking, always *add salt after cooking*—at the table, if you must. *Do not* add salt directly to food, as black dehydration spots will appear, and *no one* else will know why, and they will think you did something *else* to the food. You could add a splash of vegetable-oil margarine for flavor. I am at the point where I now eat my vegetables "straight," with nothing on them at all, because the microwave heightens vegetable flavors. So broccoli tastes more broccoli-ish and snow peas taste more of themselves. To be able to enjoy the true flavor of vegetables is a delight.

(If you must add salt before cooking, as traditional cooks often do, dissolve the salt in a small amount of water or other liquid and add to the vegetables. Remember that the microwave intensifies flavor, so salt lightly.)

Which brings me to our next vegetable, *carrots*. I selected carrots because they are different from broccoli in texture and require a different cooking technique.

Carrots are denser than broccoli. You will need to add water and cook them longer.

Scrape and wash 1½ carrots. Cut the whole carrot into

4 pieces. Cut the half carrot into ¼-inch "coins." Put all of the carrots together in the microwave-safe dish or 2-cup measure and add 1 tablespoon of water. Cover and vent with plastic wrap. Cook on High for 2 to 3 minutes. Let stand 3 minutes.

You will notice that the chunks are not as soft as the "coins." Why? Because the pieces were not all cut the same size, as we discussed earlier. Small pieces cook faster than large pieces. Next, season to your taste. For cooking times for a variety of vegetables see Appendix G.

You did it! You cooked three vegetables all by yourself.

LESSON 3: POULTRY

In this lesson, you will learn:

- to skin poultry
- placement for even cooking
- to melt margarine two ways
- the value of changing power levels
- to add color to chicken

You will need:

- chicken breast half and 1 leg
- 2 teaspoons margarine
- paprika
- paper towels
- pie plate or microwave-safe shallow dish
- 1-cup measuring cup
- wax paper

Now that you have mastered four great vegetables—broccoli, corn, potatoes, and carrots—let's move on. Your assignment will be to prepare for your family one of these four vegetables in the microwave every *other* day or night.

On the other days, you will learn more about cooking meats and poultry by following your lessons.

I hope you fall in love with the flavor of chicken and turkey and fish. These are the healthiest meats for you to eat, and they should become a mainstay of your meals.

By the time you finish this book, you will be able to cook chicken so many ways that you will be able to write a cookbook. But first, your first piece.

SKIN THAT CHICKEN

Under cold running water, wash the chicken leg and breast half and remove the skin. As you may know, you are removing the skin to remove excess fat that hides in the skin and just under it.

The easiest way to remove the skin is to start with very cold chicken—even partially frozen is helpful. (Thaw completely before cooking, however.) With a paper towel in your hand, grab the skin and pull it off—the friction of the paper towel will make it less slippery. Brute force will do it sometimes, but the paper-towel method is tried and true. In fact, if you hold a paper towel in *each* hand, it makes the piece even less slippery. If you can't get the skin off completely, don't worry, you won't be eating this piece anyway.

You could buy chicken breasts already skinned, which I do sometimes when I'm in too much a hurry to worry about the additional cost. I usually prefer to do the task myself and save the money. Tex prefers that too.

After the chicken is washed and skinned, pat it dry with a paper towel. On a pie-plate-type dish, Pyrex or other microwave-safe shallow dish, arrange the breast with the meatier part *to the outside*. On the opposite side of the dish, place the leg with the bony side *to the center*. We're *placing* this way because we know that microwaves cook the edges first, and penetrate about the first three-quarters to one-and-a-half inches of the food. We keep the leg's bony part to the center so it will not overcook.

MELTING MARGARINE

Place about a teaspoon of margarine in a 1-cup Pyrex or microwave-safe measuring cup. To melt, cook on High for 10 seconds. Notice how the margarine splatters? Now you know why, in *Save Your Heart with Susan* recipes, I melt margarine on Medium power (50 percent). A lower power eliminates the extra step of covering. The lower power takes a tiny bit longer, but cuts down on time spent covering to avoid splatters and cleaning the mess in your microwave.

Discard the melted margarine and wipe out the measuring cup you have just used. And wipe out the inside of your microwave with a cloth with warm soapy water, then rinse and dry. Use MicroCare, a cleaner (see Appendix E), if you have discovered it.

Now melt some margarine again: Put 1 teaspoon of margarine in the measuring cup. To melt, cook on Medium (50 percent) 20 seconds. See? No splatters.

(Did you have any trouble changing power levels? Did you read your Owner's Manual way back at the beginning of Chapter 5? Now would be a good time to review that material. Every microwave changes power levels differently, so it won't help for me to give you the various sequences here.)

COOKING CHICKEN

Now add a few shakes of paprika to the margarine and stir. With your pastry brush, brush *half* of the breast and *half* of the leg with this mixture. You're doing this because you want to see the color changes when the chicken is cooked. Foods cooked in the microwave have a reputation for being pale in color. You will learn how easy it is to make the chicken come out with a lovely color.

I assume your chicken breast weighs about 6 or 7 ounces (without the skin) and the leg about 2 or 3 ounces. All together you have about 8 to 10 ounces. And since chicken pieces cook at 6 to 7½ minutes per pound (remember volume and density?), this amount should take about 3 to 4½ minutes to cook on High. One last reminder. Cover the dish with wax paper. It cuts down on splatters, and holds in some heat but does not "steam" the chicken.

Sit back and relax while the chicken cooks. Or you could call someone for a three-minute conversation.

DON'T TALK TOO LONG . . . BING . . .

Aren't you excited? I know you *can't wait to open the door and see what you have cooked.* As you do, you will notice that the breast is *very* white on one side, and reddish in color on the other. Let the dish stand with the wax paper wrapped around it for 2 or 3 minutes. After the chicken stands, cut near the bone and see if the juices run clear and the meat is not pink. After standing, if the juices and the meat are still pink, cover with the wax paper and put the chicken back in the microwave for 30 seconds on High.

Why only 20 to 30 seconds? Because you do not want to *overcook* the chicken. If you overcook it, poultry will be tough and rubbery. And, of course, that's fine—I've done it and survived. So will you. Use your sense of humor here. Don't give up cooking chicken just because you overcooked it once or twice.

I remember the first time one of my chicken recipes was published in the newspaper. People would tell Tex they had tried the recipe and really liked it. Me? My recipe? They liked my recipe? I was flabbergasted. I felt the way Sally Field must have felt when she received an Oscar one year and said to the audience something along the lines of, "You really liked me!" I felt the same way. I, who *do not like to cook,* developed a recipe that was . . . good . . . I smiled all day, and you, too, should be *very proud of yourself.*

LESSON 4: MEAT

In this lesson, you will learn:

- to cook a ground-beef patty
- to add color to meat
- to prepare for and freeze a ground-beef patty
- to defrost a ground-beef patty

You will need:

- ground meat, made into two patties, one frozen for later
- browning liquid
- freezer paper or plastic wrap
- pie plate
- wax paper

The last meat to cook in this basic lesson will be a ground-beef patty. Prepare two 4-ounce patties and put a thumbprint (from your thumb) halfway through one patty so it will cook more evenly. (Microwaves penetrate rounded foods more evenly, and that is why some baked items microwaved in square baking dishes are "shielded" with foil on the corners).

Wrap the second patty in freezer paper, labeled with the name of the food, the amount, and the date. Put the patty in the freezer for the following lesson, Lesson 5.

Using the pie plate from the chicken-cooking lesson (washed, of course), place the patty in the center and brush *half* of it with a liquid-browning sauce or Worcestershire sauce. You are using either sauce for color, not for flavor.

Cook it on High for 1 to 3 minutes. This will give you a burger cooked "rare" to "medium." You probably wonder why such a large time range for such a small amount of meat (see page 113 for ranges of cooking times). The answer is that the *thickness* of the meat will determine how long to cook it. If you make it thinner, the patty will cook faster. Remember that for future cooking. You will notice the beef patty will be very juicy—much juicier than a burger made in a skillet. Mainly, I want you to see how quickly it will cook and to see if you want to brush your ground meat with browning sauce or leave it "nude." Also notice how much fat has been extracted from the patty.

LESSON 5: BREAD AND ROLLS AND MORE

In this lesson, you will learn:

- To reheat a roll
- To defrost a ground-meat patty
- Techniques for shielding

You will need:

- 1 roll
- 1 frozen ground-meat patty (from Lesson 4)
- 2 large marshmallows
- aluminum foil
- custard cup

And now on to another day and a really easy but often incorrectly prepared *reheated roll*. (The first time I reheated a roll, I cooked it for one minute. I learned the right way after that experience and subsequent trip to the dentist.)

Wrap the roll in a microwave paper towel and cook it on High for 5 to 10 *seconds*. Perfect, right? You've no doubt heard about rolls breaking teeth because they were too tough. You can do that, too, and it only takes a few more seconds. So don't add seconds carelessly. You'll need to experiment for the number of seconds needed in your microwave.

Defrosting is the second part of this lesson. Remove the beef patty from the freezer (from Lesson 4) and remove the covering. Then place the patty in the shallow pie pan. (Later, when your kitchen is better equipped, you will defrost on a utility rack).

(If the covering is stuck to the meat, you will first need to cook on high for only 10 to 15 seconds and stop. Then, open the door, remove the entire covering, and proceed with the following instructions. Removing the covering prevents "steaming" your meat.)

Program the microwave to *defrost* (30 percent or Low) for 2 minutes. Check the patty for defrosting progress to see if it is getting soft or is still hard as a rock. Can you depress it with your finger? After half of the time (1 minute), turn the patty over. When the defrosting time is finished, allow the patty to stand for 1 to 2 minutes.

After defrosting is completed, cook the beef patty the same way as in Lesson 4.

A review of defrosting tips follows. You can speed the process along if you:

- Respect *standing time*. For example, instructions for defrosting might read:
  "Defrost 5 minutes, Stand 5 minutes." Believe it. The total defrost time is actually 10 minutes, and includes the time that the microwave oven is turned off. The heat that has penetrated the first inch of food needs time to travel to the center to break down ice crystals. This equalizes the temperature throughout a piece of meat or other food. In defrosting, as in cooking, standing time is just as important as the time the microwave is on. Patience is a virtue. More defrosting tips:
- Turn the meat over halfway through the defrosting time, or pull pieces of food—like pieces of chicken—away from each other.

- Lay pieces of food flat, and don't mound them on top of each other. Stacking food will result in uneven defrosting.

The principles for *shielding* conclude Lesson 5. The instructions might sound odd, but follow them anyway.

Totally and *smoothly*, wrap one large marshmallow in aluminum foil. Place the second marshmallow in a custard cup. Put both in the microwave and cook on High 10 to 15 seconds, or until the uncovered marshmallow begins to expand. (Notice you are using a "range" in cooking time.)

Remove both marshmallows and unwrap the one covered in foil. Surprised? The one in foil looks just as it did when you put it in the microwave—uncooked. Now you see how to use foil to your advantage when you want to slow the cooking of certain parts of a food, such as the wings on a turkey. In the recipes in this book, I'll refer to this step as "Shield with foil."

Two ways to place foil over food are:

- Wrap the foil tightly around a dish, usually at the corners, as with a dish of brownies, or
- "Anchor" the foil in place with a toothpick. For example, the breast area of a turkey would be covered with foil to slow the cooking to this area.

Be sure the foil is smooth with no loose corners to attract microwave energy and is attached to the food or dish securely. Don't forget to remove the foil as your recipe directs or the food underneath will never cook!

LESSON 6: BACON

In this lesson, you will learn:

- how the microwave browns fatty foods
- about the *high* amount of fat in bacon

You will need:

- 4 strips bacon
- pie plate
- measuring cup
- paper towels

On your last day, your last piece of bacon. It's fitting. Shall we have a moment of silence? If you love the smell of cooking bacon, cooking your last piece may be difficult, but *do your best to resist.* I know the temptation is hard for some of you, but it will be worth it to save your heart. The reason I chose bacon for this lesson is so you will see how much grease accumulates and to show you that some foods do brown in the microwave. *The foods that brown quickly in the microwave are not good for your heart* because they are the same foods that are high in cholesterol and fat.

Place two strips of bacon flat on your pie plate. Cook on High for 2 to 3 minutes. (Pour the grease into a measuring cup and put it in the refrigerator. Look at it after it hardens. What you see is what cholesterol might look like in your arteries. Besides that, each *teaspoon* of fat has about 40 calories.)

Let the bacon stand 1 minute. Notice the grease clinging to the bacon. Repeat this painful bacon-cooking procedure, *except* this time place 2 microwave paper towels under the 2 slices of bacon and 2 on top. Cook on High 2 or 3 minutes. Let stand 1 minute. This time, notice that the towels have absorbed a lot of the moisture and grease and that the bacon is browned.

The lesson: Even though the bacon in the towels has less grease, each slice still has over thirty-six calories, five milligrams of cholesterol, 100+ milligrams of sodium, and over three grams of fat. Bacon is not a food that is good for our arteries, but cooking it provides some useful lessons.

GRADUATION . . . YOURS!

You laughed, you cried, you fussed and fumed. You threatened me and swore you'd give me a piece of your mind if we met. You did all of these things. And, you completed Basic 102 all by yourself.

Most important, what you learned is *some* of what I taught in my beginning microwave-cooking classes that helped beginners feel confident with the microwave. In fact, a lot of people who have been microwaving for some time may have learned some techniques in this chapter. These lessons are not intended to teach you everything about cooking in the microwave; I learn something new every time I cook. But you now know the basics and should feel confident enough to try *Save Your Heart with Susan* recipes!

The lessons don't stop here. In every recipe and many of the stories, you will find countless tips, secrets, and techniques to make microwave cooking the *best* way of cooking to save your heart.

Please award yourself the graduation diploma that follows. If you will send it to me, *in care of my publisher,* along with a self-addressed stamped envelope, I would be pleased to sign it and return it to you.

I'm proud of you. And I really mean it.

This is to certify that

_____

*has successfully completed Basic Microwaving
101 and 102 and is dedicated to learning
and cooking more in the microwave*

and is hereby awarded this

Diploma

on this _____ day of _____, 19___

_____

Susan Nicholson, R.D./L.D.

CHAPTER 10

Menus for the Rest of Your Life

๛๛๛

TV "Star"

๛ It took me a year to get up the courage to go on TV the first time. In the beginning, an Atlanta friend suggested I would be perfect for *Noonday*, an Atlanta TV daily "magazine" show. I immediately got diarrhea and felt nauseous. *No way* would I have the courage to stand in front of a *TV camera* and *cook*. I imagined TV cooking to be about a hundred times worse than regular cooking, and I wasn't wild about that.

Granted I could stand in front of an audience of five hundred, or thirty students in my cooking school and teach (*teach* stands for *talk*, which I do well) for two or more hours.

Carolyn O'Neil, the correspondent for CNN's nutrition program *On the Menu*, also gets credit for *Save Your Heart with Susan*. When I told her what I was teaching and the success I had had, she said she would like to "come out and tape the next class."

Those were the words I both craved and feared.

Now I had really done it. You all know about agony and ecstasy, I'm sure. You want *it,* but you're scared to death to get *it.* But the class was already scheduled. I made the call to Carolyn. "No problem," she said. "I'll be there with the crew about an hour before the class begins." "Great," I said weakly. Then I proceeded to go through waves of nausea.

I announced the *event* to Tex and *demanded* that he be present. I need him to be there, because no matter what an ass I might make of myself, at least he would be there to carry me out on a stretcher.

My students were "prepped" for the class, and they came dressed in their "best." I cleaned places in the store that had never seen daylight. We draped and garnished and preened. I was "wound" up with anxiety and apprehension for a week before the event.

The day came, the hour came, but CNN did not come. I called. There were temporary equipment problems. "We're waiting for you," I choked. "We're on our way," Carolyn said.

They were on their way. I was ready to pass out.

And in they came with equipment and cameras and lights and cords and people and cases. My eyes must have looked like saucers. I looked at the twenty-five students who were waiting to learn how to save their hearts.

Who's going to save my heart?

Then they wanted to interview me.

"My name? You want to know something as complicated as my name? Give me a break. Start with something easy."

Carolyn, always the professional, was patient and calming. I managed to remember my name and the benefits of using the microwave oven to cook healthy food.

Finally, I finished the fifteen-minute one-on-one interview with Carolyn, the camera, and *me.*

"Now may I leave? What? You want me to teach a two-hour class?"

And the class began.

The cameras rolled and rolled and rolled. Finally, I was in my element—performing. I just kept thinking about being a torch singer. But instead of singing "Cry Me a River," I was performing "Save Your Heart." The class went well—I could tell because I was still standing up and breathing at the end.

The next day, I could not get out of bed. For two days, I could hardly move. Miss Smarty Pants had worked herself into such a frenzy that her entire body had become a series of knots.

I went to the pharmacist and explained my problem. "Strictly tension," Steve said.

I had survived *that* TV show. Maybe I would try another TV experience. While my courage was high, I called the *Noonday* executive producer, Tracy Green. We set a date for me to appear (live). I hung up the telephone and immediately ran to the bathroom.

The first time I was on *Noonday,* I was terrified. The forty-first time I was on *Noonday,* I was terrified. I will probably be terrified the 541st time I am on TV.

The crew knew right away I was scared. I told Tracy and Paula Burton Sinkovitz (another producer) in a calm and low-key voice, "I am terrified and very nervous about this." They actually laughed. "You are the calmest terrified person we have ever had on the show. You'll do fine," they said.

Crew members continued to come over and reassure me. "It's easy," they said. "Just ignore the cameras, look and talk to the hostess, and you'll do fine."

These people crack me up. What you get is the chance to make a fool of yourself for an entire three or four minutes with no interruptions.

I soon learned that "TV food" is not like other food. You don't usually eat it, even though it might look good enough to eat. (I have a story about that, too, on page 165.)

Many of the recipes in this book were developed for the TV show. That's why they are so easy. You can't communicate simplicity in three or four minutes with a recipe that has twenty-two ingredients. If a recipe has been prepared on TV, it will have a special "TV" symbol beside it. The all-time favorite TV recipe is Banana Pudding Almost Like Mama Used to Make. That three-and-a-half-minute segment brought in hundreds of recipe requests. Be sure to try it (page 278).

About the Recipes

In the coming pages, you will find menus and recipes for more than twenty meals and almost ninety recipes. I have put dishes together that I hope appeal to you and your family and friends. Some you can prepare in advance for carefree entertaining, others you can put together at the last minute for those (frequent) times when you want dinner *now!*

Even though the recipes are grouped together in menu form, you can certainly rearrange them for your family's preferences. I haven't included recipes for tossed green salad or instructions to boil pasta on your stove, or how to prepare crusty bread—those I figure you already know. One night you will have low-fat cheese and fruit for dessert. Another night you will go out for frozen yogurt. I have tried to make the menus true to life—my life that is, and maybe yours too.

The recipes are lower in calories and low in total fat and cholesterol. Some recipes are lower in fat and sodium than others. They follow the recommendations of the U.S.

Dietary Guidelines and are recipes you can happily and healthfully live with a *long* time.

SERVES TWO HUNDRED . . .

Sometimes it is impractical to make a recipe fit exactly the number to be served. For example, if a cake serves ten and only four of you are eating, just assume you will have six pieces left over. Just because the meal is for four people, I don't want you to cut the cake into four servings. I'm watching your figure, too, you know!

WHAT'S IN A SERVING?

Each recipe includes a nutritive analysis based on a standard serving. Tex and I are hearty eaters. At our house, a recipe that may serve six to some families will feed Tex, Susan, and have a dab for leftovers. If you want to make fewer or more servings from a recipe, realize the calorie, fat, and other nutrient content will change.

IS NUTRITIVE ANALYSIS THE NEW LAW?

Nutritive analyses are *guides* at best, and all values are approximate. The "true" analysis would depend on where the food was grown, the soil the vegetables grew in, the feed the chickens ate, and even the weather. A community's water supply may vary in mineral levels, especially sodium. Of course, the sodium content of the water will affect sodium levels in the recipes. So don't live and die by nutritive count.

To get the nutrient analysis for a recipe, it's not a simple matter of punching in numbers and waiting for the computer to spit out answers. I had to estimate the nutritive breakdown for yogurt cheese for my cheesecake recipe, for example, because no "official" nutritive-analysis program available includes values for yogurt cheese as described in the recipe on page 333. Nutritive analysis is just as sketchy for drained and rinsed beans and many unsalted products.

The nutritive levels listed with each recipe do not include garnishes, optional ingredients, or ingredients "to taste."

My aim in these recipes is to give you foods you can eat over and over, and modify as you learn more about healthy eating. The whole idea of a healthy eating plan is to decrease calories and fat while increasing complex carbohydrates, fruits, and vegetables. In other words, in the world of food choices, make the healthiest ones you can make.

DESSERTS 99, BROCCOLI 3

When you compare nutrients, look at foods for what they are—*desserts have more calories than broccoli!* You really want to pay attention to: How does Save Your Heart Carrot Cake with Low-Fat Cream-Cheese Glaze compare to traditional Carrot Cake with Cream-Cheese Glaze?

30 PERCENT OF WHAT?

While an individual recipe may have a higher percentage of total fat, what else are you eating during the day? Put it all together and look at the total package. Just as no food is really "good" or "bad," no food or recipe should be singled out as an example of how you are eating.

For example, in *Save Your Heart with Susan* recipes, the overall calorie counts are quite low. And even though the grams of fat are also quite low, the lower calories make the percentage of calories from fat appear to be higher. In reality, *both* the calories *and* fat are healthfully low. Or, you might wonder about a roast-beef sandwich. The roast beef is higher in fat. But are you trimming away the fat, putting it on wholesome whole-wheat bread and cutting down or omitting mayonnaise? The combination will bring the percentage of fat calories down to a reasonable level, and give you a nutritious sandwich.

Changing your eating habits should become *The way you eat*—all of the time. I have, Tex has, Fritz and his family have. And all of us are healthier for it. As you already know, while testing recipes day in and day out for this book, both Tex and I *lost weight*. And we didn't count calories to do it—we just ate the recipes you are about to discover.

HOW TO USE THE RECIPES

A quick review of cooking terms and guidelines will help you prepare the upcoming recipes. I may not be at home when you call and need an immediate answer!

Cooking containers: All cooking containers must be microwave-safe. I don't specify microwave-safe in each and every recipe, but you must keep it in mind. Please refer to Chapter 6 for a list of approved dishes.

Covers: A cooking dish can be covered with many materials. A lid that came with the dish you are using would be a good choice, but not the only good one. Plastic wrap works well for steaming and holding in heat. See page 98. Sometimes you will see instructions that call for wax paper or paper towels to be used as a cover; each is used for specific purposes too. Again, refer to Chapter 6 for complete details.

Unless a recipe specifies that a dish remain uncovered, you should assume it is to be covered. The instructions also do not specify that covers should be vented, or opened just slightly to allow steam to escape, as a safety precaution. (Lids that come with a container have a "built-in vent.") But unless I tell you otherwise, always assume you are to vent a cover.

Blend: This means to mix ingredients together. Sometimes I will tell you to blend "to moisten," which means to mix just until the ingredients are together, but not to stir any more than is necessary. You will see "blend" in muffin recipes especially, when overstirring will cause muffins to be tough and have peaked tops and tunnels throughout.

Whisk: This utensil is used to mix ingredients. If you don't have one, put it on your "house gift" list.

Process: Put ingredients in your food processor or blender and pulse until pureed or smooth, or fine.

Skin: Take off the skin and leave the bone in. If I want you to use boneless chicken, I will specify it.

Wash: I hope it is thoroughly understood that foods need to be washed under running water (no soap please). Simple washing can neutralize a lot of problems. And don't forget your hands. Here's a toast to your health! *Bon Appétit!*

Menus and Recipes *

ત૨ત૨ત૨

Menu 1.

Happy Easter

Herbed Baked Chicken *

Parslied New Potatoes *

Steamed Asparagus * with "Un"traditional*
Hollandaise Sauce—TV *

Pineapple-Carrot Cake *
with Low-Fat Cream-Cheese Glaze—TV *

HERB-BAKED CHICKEN

SERVES 4

Can't you already taste the fat, juicy roasting hen planned for this meal? These hens aren't always available in the grocery stores, but when you can find one, the hen will weigh about 5 pounds, and have superb flavor and texture. A roasting hen will also serve more people, which might be a factor on Easter Sunday when the family gathers 'round.

If you are lucky enough to find a larger hen, simply increase the cooking time to 9 to 10 minutes per pound, and reduce the power to Medium High (70 percent). You will need to turn a larger bird once during cooking, starting it breast-side down. A smaller bird does not have to be turned and can be cooked on High for 6 to 7 minutes per pound, as in this recipe.

1 3- to 4-pound roasting chicken
1 head garlic
2 lemons, quartered
   Fresh thyme or rosemary sprigs (4 or 5 sprigs)
1 tablespoon unsalted vegetable-oil margarine
½ teaspoon liquid browning agent

1. Under cold running water, wash the chicken thoroughly, inside and out. Pat dry. Roll the garlic on a

hard surface to separate the cloves. Smash each clove with the flat side of a heavy knife, and discard the skins. Stuff the cavity with the lemon quarters and garlic.

2. Tuck the fresh herbs between the breast skin and flesh and between the skin and meat of the thigh and breast. Tie the legs together with string or a rubber band, and tuck the wings under the chicken. Place the chicken on a trivet, breast-side up, in a baking dish.

3. Put the margarine in a 1-cup measure. To melt, cook on Medium (50 percent) for 30 to 60 seconds.

4. Mix the liquid browning agent with the melted margarine and brush the chicken with half of the mixture. Cover completely with wax paper.

5. Cook on High 19 to 25 minutes, brushing with the remaining margarine mixture halfway through the cooking time.

6. Let stand 10 minutes, loosely covered with wax paper. The chicken is done when the internal temperature reaches 185 degrees F and the juices run clear when the chicken is pierced with a fork. Don't overcook; you don't want "rubber duck" for Easter!

TIP—A COUPLE OF WAYS TO PEEL GARLIC: Garlic is easier to peel if heated briefly in the microwave. For a single clove, put 1 clove on a microwave paper towel and cook on High for 15 to 20 seconds.

For a whole head of garlic, put it on a microwave paper towel. Cook on High 20 seconds, turn head upside down, and cook on High 25 seconds.

TIP: The leftover chicken makes great sandwiches.

For one serving:
Calories 139
Total fat, grams 4.8
Saturated fat, grams 1.3

Carbohydrate, grams 0
Protein, grams 24
Sodium, mg 58
Cholesterol, mg 69

PARSLIED NEW POTATOES

SERVES 4

If possible, your new potatoes (red ones) should be the size of golf balls, as they are wonderfully tender and sweet. Cut them in half; otherwise, cut larger ones into quarters or sixths.

1   **pound new red potatoes, golf-ball size**
1   **tablespoon water**
1   **tablespoon fresh parsley, chopped**
2   **teaspoons unsalted vegetable-oil margarine**

1. Scrub and cut the potatoes into 2, 4, or 6 pieces. Place them in a 4- to 6-cup measure. Add water and cover. Cook on High 6 to 7 minutes. Drain all the liquid and let stand 5 minutes, covered.

2. Put the margarine in a 1-cup measure. To melt, cook on Medium (50 percent) 30 to 60 seconds.

3. Put the potatoes in a 1-quart serving dish, pour margarine over, and toss with the parsley.

For one serving:
Calories 118
Total fat, grams 2
Saturated fat, grams 0.4

Carbohydrate, grams 23
Protein, grams 2
Sodium, mg 5
Cholesterol, mg 0

STEAMED ASPARAGUS

SERVES 4

    1   **pound fresh asparagus spears**
    3   **tablespoons water**

1. Remove the woody asparagus ends with a sharp knife, and wash the spears in cold water. Add the water to a 12″ × 8″ × 2″ dish and place the spears in the dish, with the tender tips to the center.

2. Cover and cook on High for 4 to 6 minutes. Halfway through the cooking time, move the spears in the center of the dish to the edges of the dish, still keeping buds to the center.

3. Let stand 1 to 2 minutes, covered.

TIP: Rearranging keeps delicate asparagus tips from overcooking.

For one serving: Carbohydrate, grams 5
Calories 36   Protein, grams 3
Total fat, grams 0.35   Sodium, mg 5
Saturated fat, grams .08   Cholesterol, mg 0

"UN" TRADITIONAL HOLLANDAISE SAUCE—TV*

SERVES 4

    2   **tablespoons unsalted vegetable-oil margarine**
    ¼   **cup egg substitute (or 2 egg whites)†**

*Please refer to the Kitchen Basics Chapter for larger quantities of this recipe.
† If using egg whites, add a dash or two of yellow food coloring to add color. Otherwise, the sauce will be very pale.

¼   teaspoon dry mustard
1   tablespoon fresh lemon juice
    Salt to taste
    Dash cayenne

1. Put the margarine in a 1-cup measure. To melt, cook on Medium (50 percent) 1 to 1½ minutes.

2. Add the eggs, dry mustard, lemon juice, and seasonings, and whisk thoroughly. Cook on Medium (50 percent) 45 seconds to 1½ minutes, whisking thoroughly every 30 seconds until light and thickened.

TIP: The sauce is done when it falls off the whisk in thick drops.

TIP: To get the most juice from a lemon, roll the lemon on a hard surface a couple of times, then cut it in half and cook on High for 20 seconds per half. Each half will yield about 1 tablespoon juice.

For one serving: Carbohydrate, grams 1
Calories 74   Protein, grams 2
Total fat, grams 7   Sodium, mg 30
Saturated fat, grams 1.4 Cholesterol, mg 0

PINEAPPLE-CARROT CAKE

SERVES 10

The cream-cheese glaze is wonderful poured on top of this cake. It is equally delicious poured directly into your mouth! (Ask the woman who knows.)

¾   cup cake flour
⅔   cup sugar

  1   teaspoon baking powder
 ½   teaspoon baking soda
 ½   teaspoon cinnamon
 ⅓   cup vegetable oil
  2   egg whites
 ½   cup shredded carrots
 ½   cup crushed pineapple (canned in natural juice)—
       lightly drained
 ½   teaspoon pure vanilla extract
      Chopped nuts (optional)

1. Coat a 9-inch round cake pan with vegetable-oil spray. Cut a circle of wax paper to fit inside the pan.

2. In a 4- to 6-cup measure, sift together the flour, sugar, baking powder, baking soda, and cinnamon. Add the oil and egg whites to the dry ingredients and mix 1 minute on Medium speed with an electric mixer. Fold in the shredded carrots and pineapple. Stir in the vanilla. Pour into the prepared pan.

3. Cook uncovered on Medium (50 percent) for 6 minutes. Cook on High power 2 to 4 minutes. Let stand, covered, 5 minutes.

4. Remove the cake from the pan. Glaze with Low-Fat Cream-Cheese Glaze and garnish with nuts (optional).

TIP: When baking microwave cakes, don't flour the cake pans or use the flour-fat sprays on the market. The sprays create a gummy layer on the cake.

TIP: Shredding carrots can be messy, so I shred the entire bunch at once and put them in the freezer in ½-cup portions. (A person never knows when a carrot-cake attack will occur. By having the carrots in the freezer, you're always prepared!) Drain the thawed carrots before using.

For one serving:
Calories 159
Total fat, grams 7
Saturated fat, grams 2.8

Carbohydrate, grams 22
Protein, grams 2
Sodium, mg 45
Cholesterol, mg 0

LOW-FAT CREAM-CHEESE GLAZE—TV

SERVES *10*, GLAZES ONE *8-* OR *9-INCH* CAKE

What can you say bad about powdered sugar and cream cheese?

2   ounces light cream cheese
⅓   cup powdered sugar
¼   teaspoon pure vanilla extract

1. Put the cheese in a 4-cup measure. To soften, cook on Low (30 percent) 20 to 30 seconds.

2. Add the powdered sugar and beat with an electric mixer until smooth. Stir in the vanilla extract. Spread over the cake while the cake is still warm.

For one serving:
Calories 28
Total fat, grams 1.3
Saturated fat, grams 0.8

Carbohydrate, grams 4
Protein, grams 1
Sodium, mg 22
Cholesterol, mg 4

All About Cakes

I've included a number of cake recipes in this book. I like cakes, and have been baking them since I was six years old—that was back in the scratch-only cake days. As a matter of fact, as a child my job was to bake a cake every Saturday from the time I was six or seven until I was in high school. I'm still baking them, just not as often.

At a young and tender age, I discovered that I liked cake batter almost as much as I liked the cakes themselves. My mother discovered my taste for batter as my cake layers kept getting thinner and thinner and I didn't. I was caught with the spatula in hand and the batter on face—just licking the beaters was not enough for this girl!

I was given a proper lecture in hopes that I would mend my ways. Instead, I learned to have my batter and eat my cake too—I just increased the size of the cake by one layer—two layers of batter to bake and one layer of batter to eat. Problem solved. (Yes, I was chubby.)

For a considerable number of years, I baked cakes from mixes and would still do that if it weren't for the high fat content of cake mixes, including microwave cake mixes. That's why I developed the cakes in this book—they can be made easily and inexpensively.

Now just because my cakes are healthier than conventional cakes does not mean that you are to eat the whole thing in one sitting. They still have fat and calories in them.

A few notes to make your microwave cakes a success:

1. Microwave cakes are lighter and rise higher than conventional cakes. No heat is present in a microwave oven to "hold down" the top of the cake. Of course, no crust will form for the same reason. Cakes won't brown, so plan to bake a chocolate or spice cake or frost it. If your friends turn the pan upside down to see if the cake has browned, it's time to look for some new friends.

2. Use cake flour for a better texture and a more tender cake. See page 50.

3. Because microwave cakes are so light, they dry out more quickly. Wrap leftovers carefully or freeze the extras.

4. Microwave cake recipes use less liquid than conventional recipes because the liquid doesn't have time to evaporate. Oil works much better than solid shortenings, and and that's a plus, because it is also healthier (see hydrogenation, page 48).

5. Use a pan-spray coating on your cake pan and put a circle of wax paper on the bottom to prevent sticking. Don't flour the pan or use a spray that contains flour. Flour will become gummy and leave a white paste on your cake.

6. Standing time is important in cake baking as it allows the center to complete cooking. Remove the cake from the oven when it appears slightly moist on top and the cake pulls away from the edges. Cover the cake tightly and let it sit directly on the counter to "stand." Use a toothpick to test in several places.

7. If I want a larger cake for an "occasion," I use a Bundt pan (requires enough batter for two layers). For everyday use, I bake one single layer. Whichever you choose, don't fill the pan too full. Microwave cakes rise higher and will spill over the sides. This has happened to me on several occasions.

8. Angel-food and sponge cakes don't work well in the microwave, so don't be frustrated by your failures. Of course, angel-food cake is a great heart-healthy dessert, so once in a while, when the weather is real cold outside, fire up that "other" oven and bake an angel-food cake from scratch. Just call me when you do, for it's one of my favorites.

Menu 2.

No-Time-for-Breakfast Breakfast

*Oats 'n' Apples Muffins**

*No-Time-for-Breakfast Bars—TV**

*Peachy Muffins**

*Harvest Muffins—TV**

Your Favorite Fruit Juice

Coffee or Tea

OATS 'N' APPLES MUFFINS

MAKES 10 MUFFINS

Recently, I learned that about 25 percent of Americans eat breakfast in the car. These muffin recipes were made with those road-warriors in mind. And besides being great "on-the-run food," they are low in fat and high in fiber.

The Oats 'n' Apples Muffins are sweet, and do not have the texture you expect in a muffin—they are very moist and dense. They may "stick" to your muffin papers.

They may "stick" to you too: The first time I made them, I ate 4 immediately. Try to resist! If you can resist, the muffins also freeze well.

¾ cup "processed" oat bran
1½ teaspoons baking powder
⅛ teaspoon salt (optional)
½ teaspoon apple-pie spice
¾ cup bran-flake cereal
¼ cup skim milk
1 egg white
1 tablespoon vegetable oil
½ cup applesauce, unsweetened
⅓ cup packed brown sugar
2 tablespoons raisins
2 tablespoons chopped nuts (optional)

1. Put 2 muffin papers in each cup of a muffin pan or custard cups.* Set aside.

2. In a small bowl, mix together the oat bran, baking powder, optional salt, and apple-pie spice.

3. In a 6- to 8-ounce cup measure, combine the bran-flake cereal and milk and stir until the cereal is softened, about 1 minute. Add egg white, oil, applesauce, and brown sugar. Blend 1 minute on High with an electric mixer.

4. Add the dry-ingredients mixture, stirring until ingredients are just moistened. Mix in the raisins and optional nuts.

5. Fill the muffin cups half full. Cook uncovered on High 2 to 3 minutes for 6 muffins or 20 to 30 seconds for 1. Remove when the muffins look slightly wet on top. Let stand 2 to 4 minutes or until the tops are dry.

TIP: To "process" oat bran, pulse it in your food processor until fine.

TIP: To soften brown sugar, place the opened box of brown sugar in the microwave beside a cup of water. Cook on High for 1½ minutes for half a box, or 2 to 3 minutes for a full-pound box.

For one serving: Carbohydrate, grams 23
Calories 131   Protein, grams 4
Total fat, grams 2.6   Sodium, mg 76
Saturated fat, grams 0.4 Cholesterol, mg 0

*If you are using custard cups, arrange them in a circle in the microwave.

NO-TIME-FOR-BREAKFAST BARS—TV

MAKES 16 BARS

I've been known to hate cooking so much that I never throw away food. I'll eat it myself in any shape in a New York minute. However, I would never, in a million years, give it to anyone else. So you can imagine my shock as the hostess of the TV show on which I am a regular guest picked up one of these week-old bars that I had taken in for "show," smiled into the camera, and took a bite. They looked fine for TV, but were not for eating by others.

Tex saw the tape and the look of horror on my face and fell to the floor with laughter. "You got caught, you got caught!" he yelled, wiping tears from his eyes. That embarrassing experience taught me never to take "TV food" out of the house (or let Tex see my tapes)!

4	egg whites (or ½ cup egg substitute)
2	teaspoons pure vanilla extract
1	cup dried fruit (apricots or peaches), chopped
2	cups bran-flake cereal
¼	cup golden raisins
¼	cup slivered almonds (optional)
1½	teaspoons cinnamon

1. Coat an 8-cup microwave ring pan* with vegetable oil spray and set aside.

2. Mix the egg whites and vanilla extract in a 4-cup measure and whisk until foamy. Set aside.

*Place a custard cup in the center of a 9-inch baking dish or pie plate if you don't have a ring pan.

3. In another medium bowl, combine the dried fruit, cereal, raisins, optional almonds, and cinnamon, and mix thoroughly. Add the egg mixture to the apricot mixture and blend well, mashing the cereal while stirring. Spoon the mixture into the ring pan. Pat down firmly and evenly.

4. Cook uncovered on High for 2 to 3 minutes. Let stand, uncovered, 2 minutes.

TIP: A great recipe for kids to make. It's easy!

For one serving: Carbohydrate, grams 11
Calories 53   Protein, grams 2
Total fat, grams .15 Sodium, mg 52
Saturated fat, grams .01 Cholesterol, mg 0

PEACHY MUFFINS

MAKES 8 MUFFINS

   ½   cup cake flour
   ¼   cup sugar
   ¼   teaspoon salt
   1   teaspoon baking powder
   ½   cup bran-flake cereal, finely crushed
   3   tablespoons skim milk
   1   tablespoon vegetable oil
   2   egg whites (or 1 egg), well-beaten
   ¾   cup peaches, fresh, canned in own juice, well-drained and finely chopped (or frozen and thawed)

1. Put 2 papers in each cup of a muffin pan or custard cups.* Set aside.

*If you are using custard cups, arrange them in a circle in the microwave.

2. Sift together the flour, sugar, salt, and baking powder. Place the cereal in a plastic bag and crush it almost to a powder. Add to the flour mixture and mix together.

3. In a separate container, combine the milk, oil, and beaten egg or egg whites. Stir well. Add the liquid ingredients, along with the peaches, to the dry ingredients. Stir to moisten.

4. Fill the cups half full. Cook uncovered on High 2½ to 3½ minutes for 6 muffins or 25 to 35 seconds for 1. Let stand, covered, 2 minutes.

For one serving:	Carbohydrate, grams 17
Calories 92	Protein, grams 2.3
Total fat, grams 2	Sodium, mg 138
Saturated fat, grams 0.5	Cholesterol, mg 1

HARVEST MUFFINS—TV

MAKES 8 MUFFINS

Many viewers requested this recipe after I cooked it on TV. The pumpkin adds valuable vitamin A and fiber, as well as the flavor Americans love.

- ¼   cup cake flour
- ½   cup processed oat bran
- ¼   cup wheat germ
- ⅓   cup packed brown sugar
- 1   teaspoon baking powder
- ½   teaspoon allspice
- 1   egg white, slightly beaten
- ¼   cup skim milk
- 1   tablespoon vegetable oil
- ½   cup canned or cooked pumpkin

2   tablespoons raisins
2   tablespoons chopped nuts (optional)

1. Put 2 papers in each cup of a muffin pan or custard cups. Set aside.

2. In a medium mixing bowl, mix together the flour, oat bran, wheat germ, brown sugar, baking powder, and allspice. Make a well in the center. Set aside.

3. In a separate 4- to 6-cup container, mix together the egg white, milk, oil, and pumpkin.

4. Add the liquid ingredients to the dry ingredients, and mix just enough to moisten. Fold in the raisins and nuts (optional).

5. Fill the muffin cups about half full. Cook uncovered on High 2 to 3 minutes for 6 muffins or 20 to 30 seconds for 1.

TIP: To process oat bran, pulse it in your food processor until it is fine.

TIP: To "plump" raisins or other dried fruit, place about eight ounces of fruit in a deep bowl and pour ¾ cup water over the fruit and cover. Cook on High 5 minutes, stirring after half of the time. Let stand 2 to 3 minutes. You may substitute fruit juice for the water.

For one serving: Carbohydrate, grams 20
Calories 117   Protein, grams 3
Total fat, grams 2.6   Sodium, mg 133
Saturated fat, grams 0.5   Cholesterol, mg 0

A Disclaimer on Muffins

BUT IT DOESN'T LOOK LIKE A MUFFIN

You have heard me, seen me, and read me tell you how great microwave ovens are and about all the wonderful feats you can accomplish with this fabulous machine. I hope you are brainwashed by now.

If so, this is one of those "Yes, but . . ." pauses.

The muffins in this, as well as other microwave cookbooks, are just different from what we expect from conventional oven baking. Different does not mean bad.

Muffins and breads are my two biggest microwave-cooking disappointments. Their texture is spongier and lighter than we have come to expect. Even so, I made the monumental decision to include muffins in this book. Still, I am not thrilled with microwave muffin recipes.

Cutting the fat and calories and keeping the flavor and texture provided a giant-sized challenge. If you are a food critic, and these muffins don't fit your definition of a "proper" muffin, I take the heat. As in microwave cake-baking, cake flour will give your muffins a better texture than all-purpose flour.

As using cake flour will help the texture of your muffins, using a *quick* and light hand when mixing helps the texture too. Mixing *over* 20 seconds total is likely to produce tough muffins with tunnels, because the gluten (protein) in the flour has been overly developed. Don't worry if you have a few lumps in the batter. You're supposed to.

I also know that many times you are going to be too rushed, or it's just too hot, to turn on your conventional oven. In those hot and hectic times, a microwave muffin that cooks in 20 seconds will suit just fine. And you and I, who are desperately trying to eat healthier, will sometimes sacrifice a perfect crust for the time saved. Therefore, I decided not to eliminate these muffin recipes.

TRUE CONFESSION

Tex and I eat the muffins from the recipes in this book regularly. When I made Harvest Muffins on TV, the hostess ate three and the crew polished off over a dozen in matter of minutes, so . . . give them a try. As with all microwave cooking, *do not* overcook them.

I have added "crusty" bread, rather than my own muffins, to some menus. The microwave just won't produce the dry-crust crunch we sometimes want with a meal— and it's not supposed to. For those crunchy times, turn on your other oven.

Menu 3.

Ladies' Lunch

Marie's Chicken Casserole*

Crisp Green Salad

California Muffins*

No-Guilt Chocolate Pudding—TV*

MARIE'S CHICKEN CASSEROLE

SERVES 6

My mother was a Renaissance woman. Oh, not in the sense of Amelia Earhart or Elizabeth Blackwell or any of those famous women, but one of the quiet millions who did amazing things for her time. Her accomplishments would not be very spectacular in today's world, but in 1925, riding the train from a tiny town in the Shenandoah Valley of Virginia to the far coast of Williamsburg to go to college was a bold act. I asked her once, "Mother, how did you get to college?" In her understated way, she said, "Bill Miller took me to Staunton to the train."

At William and Mary, she was exposed to the endless possibilities of the decade that began to liberate women. Her trunk, which holds many of her college clothes along with her class notes, still sits in the house our family has occupied since before 1830.

She had some friends who were right alongside her in some of her feats. One amazing accomplishment for women of her era was a cross-country trip she and four other single "girls" made in 1935. My mother, I am told, rode squeezed into the middle of the front seat—she was the shortest, and leg room was at a premium—for ten thousand miles. That was a clue to her determination! One of the women on the trip, Marie Whitmore, a lifelong friend and fabulous cook, shared with me both the following recipe for chicken casserole and a firsthand account of the "California adventure."

This recipe and menu are dedicated to those five ladies—Mary (my mother), Marie, Catherine, Grace, and Samuella. I believe I now know where some of my own determination came from . . . although if my mother were here, she would emphatically deny that it came from her *side of the family!*

2	cups cooked pasta shells (or noodles) about 2½ cups uncooked
⅓	cup green onions, thinly sliced
3	tablespoons red bell pepper, chopped
3	tablespoons unsalted vegetable-oil margarine
3	tablespoons all-purpose flour
	Salt to taste
1	teaspoon white pepper
¾	cup evaporated skim milk
¾	cup low-fat chicken stock, homemade (or broth, bouillon or consommé)
½	cup low-fat cheddar cheese, grated
2	cups cooked chicken breast, chopped
¼	cup fresh parsley, chopped
2	tablespoons toasted wheat germ for garnish

1. Cook pasta conventionally.

2. Put the green onions and red bell pepper in a 1-cup measure and cook on High for 1 to 1½ minutes, or until soft. Drain and set aside.

3. Put the margarine in a 4- to 6-cup measure. To melt, cook on Medium (50 percent) for 1½ to 2½ minutes. Add the flour, salt, and pepper and make a paste. Using

a wire whisk, gradually add the milk and then the stock, stirring constantly. Cover and cook on High 5 to 6 minutes, stirring 3 or 4 times.

4. In the meantime, in a large mixing bowl add the pasta, onions, red bell pepper, cheese, chicken, and parsley.

5. Pour the sauce over all the ingredients and mix thoroughly. Spoon into a 1½- or 2-quart casserole. Garnish with wheat germ and cover with wax paper. Cook on Medium (50 percent) for 10 minutes, or until the cheese melts and it is heated throughout.

For one serving: Carbohydrate, grams 22
Calories 266   Protein, grams 22
Total fat, grams 10   Sodium, mg 125
Saturated fat, grams 2.8 Cholesterol, mg 54

CALIFORNIA MUFFINS

MAKES 8 MUFFINS

- ¼   cup whole-wheat flour
- ½   cup cake flour
- ½   teaspoon baking powder
- ½   teaspoon baking soda
- 2   tablespoons sugar
- 1   egg (or 2 egg whites) slightly beaten
- ½   cup low-fat vanilla yogurt
- 2   tablespoons vegetable oil
- 2   tablespoons nuts, chopped (optional)

1. Place 2 papers in each cup of a muffin pan or custard cups.* Set aside.

*If you are using custard cups, arrange them in a circle in the microwave.

2. Sift together the 2 flours, baking powder, soda, and sugar in a small mixing bowl. Make a well in the center of the ingredients. Set aside.

3. In another container, combine the egg whites, yogurt, and oil. Mix well with a wire whisk. Add to the dry ingredients and mix just to moisten. Fold in the optional nuts.

4. Fill the muffin cups half full. Cook, uncovered, on High 1½ to 2½ minutes for 6 muffins, or 15 to 25 seconds for 1. The tops should be slightly moist, but do not overbake. Let stand until the tops are dry.

For one serving: Carbohydrate, grams 13
Calories 102   Protein, grams 3
Total fat, grams 4.5   Sodium, mg 106
Saturated fat, grams 1.2   Cholesterol, mg 35

NO-GUILT CHOCOLATE PUDDING—TV

SERVES 6

Puddings boil "high" in the microwave, so be sure to allow for expansion when choosing the size of your cooking dish. This is one of my most called-for TV recipes.

⅔   cup sugar
¼   cup cocoa
2   tablespoons cornstarch
2   cups skim milk
2   egg whites, (or ¼ cup egg substitute), beaten
1   tablespoon unsalted vegetable-oil margarine
1   teaspoon pure vanilla extract
    Toasted almonds or peppermint candy (optional)

1. Combine the sugar, cocoa, and cornstarch in a 6- to 8-cup measure. Gradually stir the milk into the dry mixture with a wire whisk and cover.

2. Cook on High for 5 to 8 minutes or until thickened and bubbling, stirring 2 or 3 times.

3. In a separate container, beat about half of the hot mixture into the beaten egg whites. Add this to the remaining hot mixture. Microwave on High 1 to 3 minutes or until thickened, whisking every 30 seconds. Stir in the margarine and vanilla extract. Pour into individual serving dishes or a 1-quart casserole. Place wax paper directly on the pudding, and chill.

4. Garnish with toasted almonds or crushed peppermint candy.

For one serving:
Calories 154
Total fat, grams 2.5
Saturated fat, grams 0.7

Carbohydrate, grams 28
Protein, grams 5
Sodium, mg 59
Cholesterol, mg 1.5

Menu 4.

Company's Coming!

Grilled Salmon Steaks—TV*

Company Salad*

Lemon-Rice Pilaf*

Strawberry-Banana Pie*

Crusty Bread

GRILLED SALMON STEAKS—TV

SERVES 4

Ask your butcher to cut salmon steaks that weigh about 6 ounces. Grilled salmon is always a Save Your Heart with Susan cooking-class favorite.

> 4 6-ounce salmon steaks
> 1 tablespoon olive oil
> 1 tablespoon balsamic vinegar
> 2 tablespoons fresh dill, chopped
>   Paprika for garnish
>   Sprigs of fresh dill for garnish
>   Lemon wedges for garnish

1. Preheat the browning grill according to manufacturer's instructions. In a 1-cup measure, mix the oil and vinegar together and brush one side of the salmon with the mixture. Sprinkle with dill, then paprika. When the browning grill is hot, place the salmon seasoned-side down on the grill and press down on it with a spatula. Cover with wax paper.

2. Cook on High for 4 minutes. Turn carefully. Cover with wax paper. Cook on High for 4 to 5 minutes on the second side. Let stand 1 to 2 minutes, covered.

3. When the fish is cooked, it will flake easily with a fork. To serve, place the seasoned side up, and garnish with dill sprigs and lemon wedges.

For one serving:
Calories 217
Total fat, grams 12.8
Saturated fat, grams 2

Carbohydrate, grams 1
Protein, grams 24
Sodium, mg 59
Cholesterol, mg 74

COMPANY SALAD

SERVES 4

You can change the flavor of this side dish (or en-trée) salad simply by changing the type of salad dressing you use. You can also cut calories and fat by using reduced-calorie and fat versions of your favorite dressing. The preferred flavor at our house is Thousand Island dressing, but you may like another. Eggs are listed on the label of my favorite dressing, but the amount would be so small it could be included in your four-eggs-a-week limit. But, if this bothers you, surely use another dressing that contains no eggs. Many salad dressings are now 90 percent or more fat-free (that means 10 percent fat).

Be sure that the salad dressing you use is made with unsaturated oil (see Chapter 2).

I like the bright colors of the vegetables in this salad. And the microwave is superb at "brightening" the color of vegetables. Remember, we eat with our eyes too!

¾ cup frozen green peas
1 cup fresh cauliflower, broken into flowerets
¼ cup commercial Thousand Island dressing, 90 percent or higher (or more) fat-free

1 tablespoon nonfat yogurt
3 tablespoons green onions, minced tops and bottoms
¼ teaspoon pepper
1 cup canned dark red kidney beans, rinsed and drained
½ cup spinach leaves for garnish under salad

1. Place the peas in a 1-quart casserole and cover. Cook on High 3½ minutes. Let stand 1 minute, rinse in cold water immediately, and drain. Set aside.

2. Place cauliflowerets in a 1-quart casserole and cover. Cook on High 1½ to 2 minutes. Let stand 1 minute, rinse in cold water immediately, and drain.

3. Meanwhile, in a 1-cup measure combine the salad dressing, yogurt, green onions, and pepper. Mix thoroughly.

4. In a 2-quart container, combine the cooked peas, cauliflowerets, and beans. Pour the dressing mixture over the vegetables and coat well. Cover and refrigerate several hours to blend the flavors. Serve on a bed of spinach or lettuce leaves.

For one serving:
Calories 115
Total fat, grams 2
Saturated fat, grams 0.3

Carbohydrate, grams 19
Protein, grams 6
Sodium, mg 347
Cholesterol, mg 2.4

LEMON-RICE PILAF

SERVES 4

This guide should help you determine yields for the rice recipes throughout the book.

Type of Rice	Uncooked	Liquid	Yield	Calories (1 cup cooked)
long grain	1 cup	2 cups	3 cups	223
brown	1 cup	2½ cups	3 cups	232
precooked white	1 cup	2 cups	2 cups	180

2	cups hot cooked rice (see page 295)
⅔	cup celery without leaves, thinly sliced
⅔	cup green onions with tops, thinly sliced
1	teaspoon olive oil
2	teaspoons fresh lemon juice
	Zest of one small lemon
3	tablespoons toasted pine nuts (or chopped pecans)
2	tablespoons fresh mint, chopped

1. Prepare the rice. Set aside.

2. In a 4- to 6-cup measure, mix together the celery, onions, and oil, and cover. Cook on High 2 to 3 minutes or until the vegetables are soft.

3. Put the rice in a 2-quart container. Fold in the celery/onion mixture, lemon juice, lemon zest, and nuts. Just before serving, toss with the fresh mint.

For one serving:
Calories 162
Total fat, grams 4.6
Saturated fat, grams 0.42

Carbohydrate, grams 28
Protein, grams 3
Sodium, mg 15
Cholesterol, mg 0

STRAWBERRY-BANANA PIE

SERVES 8

You won't believe how wonderful this pie tastes. If you ever thought heart-healthy food would leave you feeling deprived, this recipe will change your mind. Instead of saying no to desserts, now you can say yes!

1   baked graham-cracker crust (see page 186)
1   medium banana
3   cups fresh strawberries, stems and hulls removed
2   tablespoons sugar
2   tablespoons cornstarch
⅔   cup hot water
1   tablespoon light corn syrup
1   tablespoon (1 packet) dry, low-calorie strawberry
       gelatin dessert

1. Slice the banana into the bottom of the cooled graham cracker crust. *Slice* 2 of the 3 cups of strawberries and put them on top of the bananas. *Halve* the remaining strawberries and place them on top of the sliced strawberries.

2. Combine the sugar and cornstarch in a 1-quart casserole or glass measure. Add the water and syrup, and whisk until completely blended and cover.

3. Cook on High 1½ to 3 minutes, or until thickened. Stir several times.

4. Add the gelatin and stir until it is dissolved. Pour over the fruit in the crust and chill until firm (several hours).

For one serving: Carbohydrate, grams 23
Calories 128   Protein, grams 1
Total fat, grams 4   Sodium, mg 72
Saturated fat, grams 0.8 Cholesterol, mg 0

GRAHAM-CRACKER CRUST

MAKES 1 9-INCH CRUST

> 2   tablespoons unsalted vegetable-oil margarine
> 1   cup graham-cracker crumbs
> 2   tablespoons sugar
> ¼   teaspoon cinnamon

1. Put the margarine in a 9-inch pie plate. To melt, cook on Medium (50 percent) for 30 seconds to 1 minute.

2. Put the graham crackers in the food processor and pulse until pulverized to crumbs. Stir the crumbs, sugar, and cinnamon into the margarine. Press the mixture evenly into the pie plate.

3. Cook on High 1 to 2 minutes or until firm. Cool completely before filling.

TIP: Complete cooling keeps the crust from becoming soggy.

For one serving: Carbohydrate, grams 11
Calories 78   Protein, grams 1
Total fat, grams 3.8   Sodium, mg 71
Saturated fat, grams, 0.8 Cholesterol, mg 0

Menu 5.

Italian Night

*Save Your Heart Chicken Cacciatore
over Pasta—TV**

Fresh Summer Squash with Tarragon*

Poached Pears in Red Wine Sauce*

/

SAVE YOUR HEART CHICKEN CACCIATORE
OVER PASTA—TV

SERVES 4

Tex and I have eaten so much Save Your Heart Chicken Cacciatore, we are convinced we were Italian in another life. This recipe is always a cooking-class favorite.

½   pound pasta (cooked conventionally)
½   green bell pepper, sliced
¼   yellow bell pepper, sliced (optional)
1   16-ounce can Italian stewed tomatoes, cut up, lightly drained
1   medium yellow onion, sliced into rings
¼   cup dry white wine
½   cup fresh mushrooms, sliced (or 4-ounce can, drained)
2   tablespoons fresh oregano leaves (or 2 teaspoons dried)
1   tablespoon fresh basil, chopped (or 1 teaspoon dried)
1   tablespoon fresh parsley, chopped
4   chicken breast halves, skinned (about 2 pounds)

1. Prepare the pasta conventionally.

2. In a 6-cup or larger container, combine the green and optional yellow pepper, tomatoes, onion, wine, mush-

rooms, oregano, basil, and parsley and cover. Cook on High for 6 minutes, stirring once.

3. Arrange the chicken in a 2-quart casserole, putting the meatier portion to the outside. Spoon tomato mixture over the chicken, and cover.

4. Cook the chicken on High for 16 to 18 minutes, or until it is tender and no longer pink. Rearrange once and spoon the sauce over the chicken twice during the cooking time. Let stand, covered, 5 minutes. Serve over the cooked pasta.

TIP: Tomatoes, berries, some beans, and curry powder can stain some microwave plastic dishes. To clean the stains, combine 1 cup chlorine bleach and 1 cup water. Put the mixture into the stained dish for an hour or two. Wash the dish well with a detergent, rinse, and dry.

TIP: For a spicier dish, sweet banana peppers (available regionally) or the hotter Hungarian yellow peppers can replace the yellow bell peppers.

For one serving:	Carbohydrate, grams 25
Calories 268	Protein, grams 31
Total fat, grams 4.5	Sodium, mg 311
Saturated fat, grams 0.9	Cholesterol, mg 73

FRESH SUMMER SQUASH WITH TARRAGON

SERVES 4

- 1   medium yellow onion, cut in rings
- 1   teaspoon vegetable oil
- 4   yellow squash cut about ¼″ (about 1 pound after cutting)

1   teaspoons fresh tarragon, chopped (or ½ teaspoon
    dried)
1   teaspoon balsamic vinegar

1. Put the onion rings and oil in a 1½ or 2-quart container
   and cover. Cook on High 3 to 4 minutes, or until onions are soft.

2. Add the squash and tarragon and toss with the onions.
   Cover and cook on High for 4 to 5 minutes. Toss with
   balsamic vinegar. Let stand, covered, for 2 minutes.

For one serving:	Carbohydrate, grams 5
Calories 37	Protein, grams 1
Total fat, grams 1.4	Sodium, mg 2
Saturated fat, grams 0.3	Cholesterol, mg 0

POACHED PEARS IN RED WINE SAUCE

SERVES 4

4   ripe pears (Bosc or d'Anjou), unpeeled and uncored
¾   cup red wine
¾   cup water
½   cup sugar
1   teaspoon allspice

1. Stand the pears upright in a serving container that is at
   least 2 inches high. Set aside.

2. In a 4-cup measure, mix together the wine, water, sugar,
   and allspice, and cover. Cook on High 3 to 4 minutes
   or until boiling. Pour the sauce over the pears and cover.
   Cook on High 4 to 5 minutes or until the pears are soft.
   Let stand 5 minutes.

TIP: The pears will stand flat more easily if you remove a small slice from the bottom of the pears.

For one serving:
Calories 178
Total fat, grams 0.2
Saturated fat, grams 0.1

Carbohydrate, grams 45
Protein, grams 1
Sodium, mg 6
Cholesterol, mg 0

Menu 6.

Southern Traditions

Catfish*

Gary's True Cheese Grits*

Turnip Greens with Smoked Turkey*

Stewed Tomatoes Not-at-All-Like-They-
Served-in-Grade-School*

Peach Crisp—TV*

CATFISH

SERVES 4

Catfish of old had a bad reputation of tasting like the bottom of whichever river they came from. I heard at least one story about a man whose taste is so developed he can taste a catfish and tell you the actual river the catfish swam in! Think of what that man might do with wine.

I ate real river catfish once, and because of it, I used to deliberately avoid all catfish. But these new farm fish aren't anything like their river cousins. The farm fish have a mild flavor, and, like all fish, do very well in the microwave.

Catfish has become the rage. It's a signature dish for many trendy chefs, and some restaurants specialize in catfish the way others do lobster. The Wooden Lamb, a restaurant near my hometown, comes to mind for its wonderful catfish.

The recipe I have devised is so easy, it's embarrassing, but then, my recipes are all easy.

1	pound farm-raised catfish fillets
½	cup skim milk
¼	teaspoon cayenne pepper
¼	teaspoon black pepper
¼	teaspoon salt
1	tablespoon dry bread crumbs

3   tablespoons yellow cornmeal
Lemon slices to garnish

1. Place the catfish in an $8'' \times 12'' \times 2''$ baking dish. Pour
   the skim milk over the catfish. Cover and refrigerate
   for 30 minutes to several hours.

2. In a plastic bag, mix together the cayenne pepper, black
   pepper, salt, bread crumbs, and cornmeal. Place a paper towel on a utility rack. Set aside. Remove the catfish from the milk and drain them well. Pat dry and
   coat them in the cornmeal mixture and place them on
   the utility rack. Top them with another paper towel.

3. Cook on High 3 to 5 minutes. Let stand 3 minutes, covered. Fish is done when it is opaque and flakes easily
   with a fork. Garnish with lemon slices.

TIP: To keep fish extra moist during cooking, first coat them
in beaten egg white, then in a mixture of toasted wheat
germ and cornmeal before baking.

For one serving: Carbohydrate, grams 7
Calories 161   Protein, grams 22
Total fat, grams 5   Sodium, mg 224
Saturated fat, grams 1.2   Cholesterol, mg 66

GARY'S TRUE CHEESE GRITS

SERVES 4

*True or False: Everybody in the South loves grits
and eats them all the time. Some of you probably
answered a resounding True to that question. But
this book was written by a Virginia/Texas/Georgia
"girl" who had to leave Virginia to become ac-*

quainted with grits. So, the answer to the above question is False.

However, you won't get off so easily, because I have several grits stories.

The first person, and as far as I know the only person, in my hometown who ate grits regularly was a Mr. Dee Wilson. I know he ate them because, as a high school student, I worked as a waitress in his (now closed) restaurant, Don Dee's. Every day the cook made grits for Mr. Wilson.

Judy, my best friend, and I worked summers at Don Dee's Court, and every summer morning, Mr. Wilson ordered grits for breakfast. One morning, when no one was looking, we each stuck a finger in the bowl of grits to see just what the attraction might be. To our uneducated palates, they tasted just like wallpaper paste.

I never did find out how great grits could be until I left Virginia for Texas. Tex's brother, Gary, once baked some True Cheese Grits for us. Now his grits were interesting.

This is a knock-off, and a tribute to Gary's Grits. I add chopped jalapeño peppers for me, but Tex can't take the heat. (He says he's from Texas, but who ever heard of a Texan who couldn't take the heat?) You can decide what your family prefers.

1 cup quick-cooking grits
3 cups hot water
  Salt to taste
¼ teaspoon pepper
½ teaspoon cayenne pepper
¼ cup low-fat cheddar cheese, shredded
½ canned hot jalapeño pepper, seeded and chopped

1. Combine the grits, water, salt, black pepper, and cayenne pepper in a 2- or 3-quart casserole. Cook, uncovered, on High, 8 to 10 minutes. Stir once.

2. Add the cheese and jalapeño peppers and stir. Cover and let stand 1 to 2 minutes or until cheese melts.

For one serving: Carbohydrate, grams 31
Calories 188   Protein, grams 9
Total fat, grams 3   Sodium, mg 309
Saturated fat, grams 1   Cholesterol, mg 0

TURNIP GREENS WITH SMOKED TURKEY

SERVES 4

Growing up in Virginia, I entered the "green" world through kale and spinach. These two aren't like the delicate salad lettuces that are called greens by many cooks. These hardier vegetables can take a little "wilting," meaning that we poured hot bacon grease and vinegar over them.

My horizons were vastly broadened when I moved to Texas and worked as a VA hospital dietitian. Menu planning was part of my job. I worked with a dietitian who was a native Texan. My friend Martha and I found if we wanted a winning meal, all we had to do was combine catfish and greens— the patients and staff would love us. (Hospital dietitians need love too.)

Martha knew all about greens, but I had to be taught. I learned that most Texans would eat greens (any kind except kale, which no one in Texas had heard of) for breakfast, lunch, and dinner, as long as they were cooked the right way. "Cooked right" meant, of course, that these vitamin-filled wonders had the begeebees cooked out of them until they were nutritious wonders no more.

Over the years, I, too, have become a big "green" fan, but certainly not a great "green" cook. And then Save Your Heart with Susan came along. I knew I had to include greens, somehow. They are central to southern cooking, and the menu following wouldn't be complete without them. But overcooking greens with ham hocks or bacon or fatback to produce an ocean of thick fatty pot "likker," had to go.

Along came the idea of cooking greens in the microwave and replacing the standard bacon with a different smoked meat that was lower in fat. Off to the grocery store I went, cart and notebook in hand.

I followed shoppers around and looked in their carts. If I saw greens, I started asking questions. I took a survey of the "preferred" greens, and a survey of the "preferred" cooking methods.

I soon learned that greens are just like everything else: Everyone has his favorite. There was no consensus. Mustard, collard, or turnip greens all have a loyal following.

Next, I followed a woman buying greens across the store until we ended up in front of the smoked-turkey counter. "Aha," I said, "now I know what to do," and I was so excited over my discovery that I raced out of the store, barely stopping at the cashier's post.

Before cooking, wash the greens well, and I mean well. *One friend even suggested using a washing machine with cold water, and one swore that all greens were top-rack safe in the dishwasher. I've had no experience in either method. My boring sink gets all my greens.*

Fill the sink with cold water, and rinse and wash away the sand and dirt. Let the sink drain, and fill it again. Repeat this step several times. Don't pour the used water over the greens if you wash them in a big bowl—you would be "reinfecting" them with dirty water. After rinsing several times, wash both sides of each leaf under cold running water to remove any remaining grit.

When the greens were cooked, Tex took one bite, got a great big smile on his face, and said, "These are good," and you know where he is from, so he must be an expert. I'm proud of this recipe, and I hope you like it too.

1	teaspoon olive oil
1	cup yellow onions, chopped
1	garlic clove, minced
4	ounces smoked turkey breast (or other parts), skinned and cut up
1	cup low-fat chicken stock, homemade (or broth, bouillon or consommé)
¼	teaspoon crushed red pepper flakes (or 6 drops Tabasco sauce)
1	teaspoon sugar
1	pound fresh turnip (or collard) greens, washed and cut into thin strips

1. Mix together the oil, onions, and garlic in a 2-cup measure. Cover and cook on High 2 minutes or until the onions are soft. Set aside.

2. In a 3- or 4-quart container, place the turkey, stock, red pepper, and sugar. Cover and cook on High 5 to 7 minutes or until boiling. Then cook on Low (30 percent) for 10 minutes.

3. Meanwhile, clean the greens. When the turkey has finished cooking (in previous step), add the greens and the onion/garlic mixture. Cook on High 20 to 25 minutes. Let stand, covered, 5 minutes.

TIP: If you choose mustard greens, cook them twice as long.

For one serving:

Calories 99

Total fat, grams 2.5

Saturated fat, grams 0.6

Carbohydrate, grams 9

Protein, grams 10

Sodium, mg 59

Cholesterol, mg 0

STEWED TOMATOES NOT-AT-ALL-LIKE-THEY-SERVED-IN-GRADE-SCHOOL

SERVES 4

Now you might surely wonder why I named this recipe as I did. It's like this: Practically everyone I ever talked to (at least everyone over the age of thirty-five) had some memory of "stewed tomatoes" served in the elementary-school cafeteria. None of the memories were what we would call "fond."

The tomatoes that follow are nothing like the ones from the old days. I'm sure to hear from all my friends in school food service after this, so for all of you elementary-school survivors, I am "braced." Here goes. . . .

1 small yellow onion, chopped

1 teaspoon olive oil

1 16-ounce can stewed tomatoes, drained slightly

1 tablespoon sugar

1 tablespoon fresh basil, chopped (or 1 teaspoon dried)

2 tablespoons cornstarch

2 tablespoons cider vinegar

1 tablespoon toasted wheat germ

1. Combine the onion and oil in a 1-quart baking dish and cover. Cook on High 2 to 3 minutes, or until the onions are soft.

2. Add the tomatoes, sugar, and basil, and stir. Cook, uncovered, on High 2 minutes.

3. Mix the cornstarch and the vinegar in a 1-cup measure until smooth. Stir it into the tomato mixture, and cover. Cook on High 2 minutes, stirring once. Let stand 2 minutes, covered. Stir again. Top with the toasted wheat germ.

For one serving:
Calories 98
Total fat, grams 1.4
Saturated fat, grams 0.2

Carbohydrate, grams 17
Protein, grams 2
Sodium, mg 244
Cholesterol, mg 0

PEACH CRISP—TV

SERVES 4

    3   cups fresh peaches,* sliced (or frozen, unsweetened
            and thawed peaches)
    ¼   cup raisins
    ¾   teaspoon nutmeg
    1   tablespoon fresh lemon juice
    3   tablespoons packed brown sugar
    ¼   cup whole-wheat flour
    ¼   cup oatmeal
    2   tablespoons chopped pecans (optional)
    2   tablespoons unsalted vegetable-oil margarine

1. Drain the peaches. Reserve 4 slices for garnish. Mix together the raisins, nutmeg, and lemon juice. Add to the peaches and spread them evenly over the bottom of a 9-inch baking dish. Set aside.

---

*If you use canned peaches, drain them thoroughly.

2. In a small bowl, combine the brown sugar, flour, oatmeal, and optional pecans. Cut in the margarine to form coarse crumbs. Spread this mixture over the fruit mixture.

3. Cook, uncovered, on High 5 to 8 minutes or until peaches are tender and mixture bubbles around the edges. Garnish with reserved slices.

For one serving: Carbohydrate, grams 32
Calories 187   Protein, grams 2
Total fat, grams 6.0   Sodium, mg 8
Saturated fat, grams 1   Cholesterol, mg 0

Menu 7.

I'm Starving—
Let's Eat!

Dinner-in-a-Dish*

Mixed Green Salad

Honey Oat-Bran Muffins*

Plate of Apples and Grapes

DINNER IN A DISH

SERVES 4

You're tired. The family is tired. Everyone is grouchy. And even if you could afford it, who has the energy to get the family packed into a car and into a restaurant? Better to stay at home, put on your bathrobe, put the kids in the tub, and throw a batch of "stuff" together. Luckily, when you throw this batch of "stuff" together, it tastes good and feels comforting. Afterward, there are, count them, two pots to wash. Amen.

¾ cup yellow onion, chopped
½ pound ground round (or turkey)
1 cup elbow macaroni, uncooked
1 15-ounce can stewed tomatoes, chopped, with
       liquid
1 8-ounce can tomato sauce, no salt added
1 cup frozen whole-kernel corn, thawed
1 teaspoon packed brown sugar
1 teaspoon chili powder
¼ teaspoon cumin
1 cup water
   Salt to taste
½ teaspoon pepper
1 tablespoon balsamic vinegar
¼ cup low-fat cheddar cheese, shredded

1. Place the onions in a colander, set inside a 2-quart dish and cover. Cook on High 2 to 3 minutes, or until soft. Add the ground meat. Cook on High 2½ to 3 minutes or until meat is no longer pink, stirring once. Discard the grease and liquid that has collected in the bottom pan. Put the meat/onion mixture in the bottom container.

2. Add the macaroni, tomatoes with liquid, tomato sauce, corn, brown sugar, chili powder, cumin, water, salt, and pepper to the meat mixture. Mix well and cover. Cook on High 17 to 19 minutes. Stir after half the cooking time. Stir in the balsamic vinegar. Let stand, covered, 10 to 12 minutes. Stir before serving, then garnish with cheese.

For one serving:
Calories 433
Total fat, grams 9
Saturated fat, grams 3.1

Carbohydrate, grams 67
Protein, grams 21
Sodium, mg 354
Cholesterol, mg 33

HONEY OAT-BRAN MUFFINS

MAKES 6 MUFFINS

I really "stewed" over this recipe. No self-respecting book on saving your heart could get published without an oat-bran muffin recipe. For a long time, I thought this book was going to be a "first" in that category. Like so many others, I took the oat-bran story to heart and tried valiantly to develop a benchmark recipe. I got sawdust rocks instead.

I had about given up creating a recipe that I could recommend to you. Then, a bona fide expert sent me her recipe. Which expert? My sister-in-law, Loretta. Her healthy cooking keeps one heart "saved"—my brother Fritz's, that is.

I've made some adjustments in ingredients for the microwave, but you can thank Loretta for not letting me give up. You might also add a half-cup of pureed fruit. Some of Loretta's friends use applesauce, and sometimes baby-food fruit, which is pureed and pure.

1	cup plus 2 tablespoons "processed" oat-bran cereal
2	tablespoons packed brown sugar
1½	teaspoons baking powder
¼	teaspoon salt (optional)
2	egg whites (or ¼ cup egg substitute), beaten
¼	cup skim milk
2	tablespoons honey
1	tablespoon vegetable oil
2	tablespoons raisins
2	tablespoons chopped nuts (optional)

1. Place 2 muffin papers in a muffin pan or custard cups.*
   Set aside.

2. Combine the oat bran, brown sugar, baking powder, and salt in a 4- or 6-cup mixing bowl. In another small bowl, beat the egg whites until foamy, and to the eggs add the milk, honey, and oil, and mix.

3. Add the wet ingredients to the dry ingredients, and mix just until moistened. Do not overmix. Fold in the raisins and (optional) nuts.

4. Fill the muffin cups half full. Cook, uncovered, on High 2 to 3 minutes for 6 muffins, or 20 to 30 seconds for 1. Let stand 2 minutes.

*If you are using custard cups, arrange them in a circle in the microwave.

TIP: To process oat bran, pulse it in your food processor until fine.

For one serving:
Calories 140
Total fat, grams 3.5
Saturated fat, grams 0.6

Carbohydrate, grams 22
Protein, grams 4
Sodium, mg 97
Cholesterol, mg 0.2

Menu 8.

Dinner for One and Liking It

Spring Chicken with Vegetables—TV*

"Herby" Corn*

Low-Cholesterol Cookies

SPRING CHICKEN WITH VEGETABLES—TV

SERVES 1

Thelma Pressman taught me a lot about cooking in the microwave, and one of my favorite tips is how to cook in microwave paper towels—the ultimate in easy cleanup. This recipe was a TV favorite.

1   white microwave paper towel
½   medium carrot, cut julienne style
2   golf-ball-sized red potatoes, sliced ¼" but not skinned
1   green onion, thinly sliced
½   medium zucchini, cut julienne-style
1   chicken breast half, boned and skinned (4 or 5 ounces)
⅛   teaspoon ground ginger
2   teaspoons fresh thyme (or ½ teaspoon dried)
¼   cup apple juice (or white wine)

1. Place the paper towel flat on an 8- to 10-inch round glass baking dish or pie plate. Layer the vegetables on the towel with the carrots on the bottom, then the potato, onion, and zucchini. Top with the chicken breast. Season with ginger and thyme.

2. Wrap the paper towel around the chicken, and pour the apple juice over the "bundle." Cook on High 4 to 6 minutes, or until chicken is no longer pink. Let stand 1½ minutes wrapped.

For one serving:
Calories 306
Total fat, grams 4
Saturated fat, grams 1

Carbohydrate, grams 39
Protein, grams 28
Sodium, mg 82
Cholesterol, mg 65

"HERBY" CORN

SERVES 1

Necessity sometimes creates the best recipes. One day, in the midst of writing this book, I was desperate for "something" to eat with my standard turkey-sandwich lunch. The day was one of those when the refrigerator looked as if no one really lived in this house and ate here. All I could find was one leftover ear of cooked corn on the cob.

Waste not, want not, the saying goes. Problem one solved, but I didn't want the messiness that goes with corn on the cob. To the spice rack I ran. I found just the thing—a variety of seasonings developed by the American Heart Association (AHA). The three varieties I found were Lemon Herb, "Original" Herb, and Salad Herb, and they can be used on almost any kind of food.

Out came my knife, off went the kernels of corn into a bowl. And the rest follows.

1   ear of corn on the cob, cooked
1   teaspoon AHA Herb Seasoning
1   teaspoon unsalted vegetable-oil margarine

1. Cut the kernels from the cob and put them in a 2-cup measure and cover. Cook on Medium High (70 percent) 2 to 3 minutes. Add seasoning and margarine. Stir and cover. Let stand 1 minute.

For one serving:
Calories 100
Total fat, grams 4.2
Saturated fat, grams 0.8

Carbohydrate, grams 14
Protein, grams 2
Sodium, mg 3
Cholesterol, mg 0

LOW-CHOLESTEROL COOKIES

More and more varieties and flavors of low-cholesterol, low-fat cookies are appearing in many grocery stores. Always read the label carefully.

Menu 9.

Summer in the City

Steamed Artichokes—TV*

Sole with Fresh Tomatoes and Basil Sauce*
over Herb Pasta

French Bread

Bill Adler Bars*

STEAMED ARTICHOKES—TV

SERVES 4

According to the Castroville Artichoke People, in Castroville, California, the best artichokes for the microwave are the green globe artichokes with thorns. Thornless artichokes' genetic makeup causes them to have mushy bottoms and inedible leaves when cooked in the microwave. The Artichoke People recommend the following cooking method:

4   green globe artichokes
4   teaspoons fresh lemon juice
¼   cup water
3   tablespoons vegetable-oil margarine (optional)
3   teaspoons fresh lemon juice (optional)

1. Soak the artichokes in cold water for 30 minutes.

2. Trim the artichokes 1 inch at the tops and about 1 to 1½ inches on the bottoms. Remove the small lower leaves. Using sharp scissors, snip off the tips of the leaves. Brush the cut edges with lemon juice to prevent darkening.

3. Place the artichokes upside down in a deep baking dish. Add water and cover. Cook them on High 10 to 14 minutes (or see the chart below). Let stand, covered, 3

minutes. When a toothpick can be easily inserted in the stem ends, the artichokes are done.

	Water
1 artichoke—4 to 5 minutes	1 tablespoon
2 artichokes—6½ to 8 minutes	2 tablespoons
4 artichokes—10 to 14 minutes	¼ cup

4. To melt the (optional) margarine, put the margarine in a 2-cup measure and cook on Medium (50 percent) for 1½ to 2½ minutes. Stir in the lemon juice. The margarine may be served as a dipping sauce with the artichokes.

For one serving:	Carbohydrate, grams 13
Calories 66	Protein, grams 3
Total fat, grams 0.2	Sodium, mg 79
Saturated fat, grams .05	Cholesterol, mg 0

SOLE WITH FRESH TOMATOES AND BASIL SAUCE OVER HERB PASTA

SERVES 4

My family never ate fish when I was growing up. As the story goes, my father, who went on annual fishing expeditions and brought home plenty of fish, had no intention of eating them. Of course, my mother would prepare the fish (you guessed it— fried) and when supper was about to be served, my father would telephone to say he had a "last minute" meeting, and that the family should go ahead and eat without him.

We all knew what had actually happened. My father had driven by the house and thought he could

*smell the cooking fish. Then he drove to the near-
est telephone and called to tell my mother about
the "meeting."*

*Do you think anyone with that kind of training
would ever have healthy arteries? We didn't know
any better then. But lucky us—we do now.*

1	pound herb pasta
2	medium fresh tomatoes, peeled and chopped coarsely
1	tablespoon fresh basil, chopped (or 1 teaspoon dried)
¼	teaspoon sugar
2	teaspoons unsalted vegetable-oil margarine
¼	cup green onions with some tops, chopped
1	clove garlic, minced
1	tablespoon fresh lemon juice
	Salt to taste
¼	teaspoon white pepper
1	pound sole fillets (or flounder, scrod, orange roughy)

1. Prepare the pasta conventionally.

2. Combine the tomatoes, basil, and sugar in a small bowl.
   Toss gently and set aside. Put the margarine in a separate 4- to 6-cup measure. To melt, cook on Medium
   (50 percent) for 10 to 20 seconds. Add the onions, garlic,
   lemon juice, salt, and pepper, stir and cover.

3. Cook on High 1 to 2 minutes, or until the onions are
   soft. Add the drained tomato mixture to the onion mixture, cover, and set aside.

4. Pat the fish dry with paper towels and place them in
   an 8″ × 12″ × 2″ baking dish. Fold under the thinner ends
   for more even cooking and cover. Cook on High 3 to 4
   minutes, or until the fish just turns opaque and flakes.

5. While the fish stands, cook the vegetables (from step 2) on High 1 to 2 minutes, or until heated throughout. To serve, spoon vegetables over the fish.

TIP: Peeling fresh tomatoes is easy, using your microwave as a helper. Cut an X in the bottom of each tomato and place in the microwave on a microwave paper towel. For room-temperature tomatoes, cook on High 30 seconds for 1 tomato. For chilled tomatoes, cook on High 1½ minutes for 1 tomato. Let stand 10 minutes and peel off the skin.

For one serving:	Carbohydrate, grams 20
Calories 224	Protein, grams 27
Total fat, grams 4	Sodium, mg 109
Saturated fat, grams 0.7	Cholesterol, mg 68

BILL ADLER BARS

MAKES 16 BARS

After months of testing recipes, I declared I had tested my last. Never say never, I learned in my adult life—these bars turned out to be so delicious, I couldn't deprive you of just one more dessert.

The perfect name is in honor of my agent, who knows of what he speaks—"Susan, once you write a book, your life will never be the same."

Bill, do you know everything about everything? You sure knew about my life.

I'm going to watch this guy!

⅓ cup packed brown sugar
3 tablespoons light corn syrup
2 tablespoons unsalted vegetable-oil margarine
2 egg whites

>   ¾   teaspoon grated orange peel
>   ¾   teaspoon pure vanilla extract
>   ½   cup cake flour
>   ½   cup wheat germ
>   ½   cup quick-cooking oatmeal
>   ½   teaspoon baking powder
>   ⅓   cup raisins
>   ¼   cup chopped almonds (optional)

1. Coat an 8-cup ring pan* with vegetable-oil spray. Set aside.

2. Put brown sugar, corn syrup, and margarine in a 4- to 6-cup measure. Blend well with an electric mixer. Add the egg whites, orange peel, and vanilla extract, and continue blending with the mixer until well mixed.

3. In a small bowl, combine the flour, wheat germ, oatmeal, and baking powder, mixing them together with a whisk.

4. Gradually add the dry ingredients to the sugar mixture, blending well with an electric mixer. Stir in the raisins and nuts. (The batter will be stiff.)

5. Spread the mixture evenly in the prepared pan. Cook, uncovered, on Medium (50 percent) 4 to 5 minutes. Let stand, covered 5 minutes. Cool and cut into 16 bars. Store tightly covered.

For one serving: Carbohydrate, grams 17
Calories 90   Protein, grams 3
Total fat, grams 2   Sodium, mg 23
Saturated fat, grams 0.34   Cholesterol, mg 0

*If you don't have a ring or Bundt pan, place an inverted custard cup in the center of a round two-quart baking dish.

Menu 10.

Eat Your Vegetables (and Fruit)

Melting-Pot Lentils* served over
Steamed Brown Rice*

Zucchini Boats*

Apple-a-Day Cake—TV*

MELTING-POT LENTILS

SERVES 4

Wendy and Susan; Susan and Wendy. Where you see one, the other is surely close behind. They are best friends and opposites—isn't that always the way? They also own a microwave store and cooking school together.

They both love to cook and are great at both cooking and eating. Food is high on their list of favorite topics. Want to know the best and latest restaurant anywhere? Call on one of them. Want to know how to cook something? Give 'em a ring. Now you know one of the reasons I'm telling you about this pair.

Knowing I was writing this book and knowing my sometimes lack of enthusiasm for kitchen chores, they sent me stacks of recipes they had developed. (They were afraid of what I might do otherwise, I think). I tested theirs and turned them into save-your-heart wonders. Some of my favorites are included in this book. So when you see Wendy/Susan in the heading, you know that the San Raphael, California, team had a part in saving your heart.

When you're in the area, drop by their store (see Appendix F). They will probably invite you to dinner.

2   teaspoons olive oil
1   stalk celery without leaves, chopped
1   garlic clove, minced
½   cup fresh parsley, chopped
1   yellow onion, chopped
2   tablespoons sun-dried tomatoes, chopped
1   (or ½) canned medium hot jalapeño pepper, seeded and chopped
3   cups low-fat chicken stock, homemade (or broth, bouillon or consommé)
¾   cup dried lentils

1. Combine the oil, celery, garlic, parsley, onion, tomatoes, and jalapeño pepper in a 2- to 3-quart casserole. Mix thoroughly and cover.

2. Cook on High 4 to 6 minutes or until the vegetables are softened. Add the stock and the lentils and stir. Cook on High 20 to 30 minutes, uncovered, or until the lentils are tender. Serve over brown rice.

TIP: To reheat leftovers, cook on Medium High (70 percent) for 1½ minutes per cup of food.

For one serving: Carbohydrate, grams 13
Calories 108   Protein, grams 5
Total fat, grams 4   Sodium, mg 75
Saturated fat, grams 0.5   Cholesterol, mg 0

STEAMED BROWN RICE

SERVES 4

Make brown rice a great/healthy/filling/fabulous complex-carbohydrate staple in your new healthy eating plan. It is high in soluble fiber, protein, and vitamin E.

Brown rice takes just as long to cook in the microwave as it does the other way, but like other rice, in the microwave it always works. I cook large amounts and freeze the leftovers in 1-cup quantities. That way, I always have rice when I need it, and it won't slow down meal preparation. To boost the flavor, you may use chicken stock for all or part of the liquid.

One cup of uncooked brown rice equals 3 cups cooked.

> 1   cup brown rice
> 2½   cups hot water
> 1   teaspoon salt (optional)

1. In a 3-quart container, combine the rice, water, and salt and cover. Cook on High 5 minutes, or until boiling.

2. Reduce power to Medium (50 percent) and cook 30 minutes, or until the liquid is absorbed.

3. Let stand, covered, 5 minutes.

For one serving: Carbohydrate, grams 37
Calories 173   Protein, grams 4
Total fat, grams 0.75   Sodium, mg 0
Saturated fat, grams 0.2   Cholesterol, mg 0

ZUCCHINI BOATS

SERVES 4

Susan and Wendy shared this recipe too. I added the extra herbs.

¼   cup celery without leaves, chopped finely
¼   cup green bell (or red) peppers seeded and chopped

½   cup yellow onion, chopped
1   teaspoon olive oil
2   medium zucchini, halved lengthwise
½   cup mushrooms, sliced
1   tablespoon fresh oregano, thyme, or basil, chopped
        (or 2 teaspoons dried)
    Salt and pepper to taste
¼   cup Italian Pasta Topper* (Formagg brand)

1. Combine the celery, peppers, onion, and oil in a 4-cup measure and cover. Cook on High 3 minutes. Stir once.

2. Remove the pulp from the zucchini, chop, and place it in a mixing bowl, leaving the emptied shells for stuffing. Add the mushrooms, herb, salt, and pepper. Add the zucchini mixture to the celery mixture. Fill the emptied zucchini shells, dividing the mixture equally among the 4 halves. Place them in a flat baking dish.

3. Cook, uncovered, on High for 4 minutes. Top with the cheese. Cook on Medium High (70 percent) for 1 minute, or until the cheese is melted. Let stand 1 minute.

TIP: This dish can be made spicier by using Italian "frying" peppers or other "warmer" peppers, such as Poblanos or Anaheims in place of the green bell pepper. When a recipe calls for yellow bell peppers or banana peppers (available regionally) and you want to add some "zing," try the hotter Hungarian yellow peppers.

For one serving: Carbohydrate, grams 6
Calories 57   Protein, grams 3
Total fat, grams 2.3   Sodium, mg 73
Saturated fat, grams 0.4   Cholesterol, mg 0

*If this low-fat cheese is unavailable in your area, use Parmesan cheese. The same amount of Parmesan cheese has more calories, fat, cholesterol, and sodium.

APPLE-A-DAY CAKE—TV

SERVES 10

One of the treats of being a TV "star" is that I am often on the show with real *stars. The day I made Apple-a-Day cake on TV, Stacy Keach, of* Mike Hammer *fame, was a guest. He was in town with the touring cast of* The King and I. *What a nice guy (and a hunk!). He autographed the recipe and loved the cake. Now, if Mike Hammer liked it, I guarantee you will. I think this is one of the best cakes I ever put in my mouth. A viewer of my cooking segment put it even better. She said:*

"Susan: I took your Apple-a-Day Cake to a surprise party and everyone was crazy about my simple dessert. Donna."

See what you think.

⅔   cup packed brown sugar
½   cup vegetable oil
1   cup applesauce, unsweetened
1   cup cake flour
1   teaspoon baking soda
½   teaspoon cinnamon
½   teaspoon nutmeg
¼   teaspoon cloves
¼   cup raisins
¼   cup nuts, chopped (optional)
    Powdered sugar (optional)

1. Coat a 9-inch round cake pan with vegetable-oil spray. Place a circle of wax paper in the bottom of the pan to prevent sticking. Set aside.

2. In a medium mixing bowl, blend the brown sugar and oil until smooth. Add the applesauce and blend thor-

oughly. In a separate bowl, sift together the flour, soda, cinnamon, nutmeg, and cloves. Add the dry ingredients to the oil mixture and mix 1 minute on Medium speed with an electric mixer.

3. Add the raisins and optional nuts and blend with a spoon. Pour into the prepared pan. Cook, uncovered, on Medium (50 percent) for 6 minutes, then, cook on High 2½ to 5 minutes. Let stand, covered, 5 minutes.

4. After the cake has cooled, "dust" the top with powdered sugar.

For one serving:
Calories 219
Total fat, grams 11
Saturated fat, grams 2.8

Carbohydrate, grams 28
Protein, grams 2
Sodium, mg 101
Cholesterol, mg 0

Menu 11.

Summer Grill

*Indoor/Outdoor Grilled Chicken**

*Corn-on-the-Cob—TV**

*Sliced Red and Yellow Tomatoes Sprinkled
with Balsamic Vinegar and Herbs*

*What's-her-name's Baked Beans**

*Mrs. Raney's Wacky Cake—TV**

INDOOR/OUTDOOR GRILLED CHICKEN

SERVES 6

This "combination" cooking method not only speeds up the cooking time, but the initial microwave cooking extracts extra fat from the meat, giving you leaner chicken.

¾ cup commercial 90 percent or more fat-free Italian dressing for marinade
6 chicken breast halves, skinned (about 2½ to 3 pounds)

1. Put the chicken breasts in a heavy "resealable" plastic bag. Add the marinade and turn to coat the chicken thoroughly. Place the bag in a casserole dish for easier handling. Refrigerate 4 to 10 hours or overnight, turning the bag a few times to distribute the marinade.

2. Preheat the outdoor grill. Meanwhile, remove the chicken from the marinade (reserve for later) and place it on a utility rack, with the meatier portions toward the outside. Cover with wax paper. Cook on High 2 to 2½ minutes per chicken breast half.

3. When the grill is ready, position the grilling rack 4 to 6 inches from the coals. Place the chicken meatier side down on the grilling rack and grill 10 minutes on the

first side. Brush with the reserved marinade and turn. Grill 5 to 7 minutes on second side, or until chicken is no longer pink.

For one serving: Carbohydrate, grams 1
Calories 157   Protein, grams 27
Total fat, grams 5   Sodium, mg 220
Saturated fat, grams 1   Cholesterol, mg 74

CORN ON THE COB—TV

Just those words bring visions of my father's garden. He's over eighty now, but still, each summer he all but forgets the family business of selling cars, and devotes himself to the care and nurturing of tomatoes, corn, and other wonders of the summer soil. Even today, as soon as the first tomatoes and corn are harvested, he sends me a UPS box of the vine-ripened and juicy red and yellow beauties.

Corn is one of his specialties. It's also a wonderful food for a heart-healthy diet—full of vitamins, minerals, complex carbohydrates, and fiber. And don't worry about putting butter on it: One friend of mine was invited to a neighbor's house for a dinner of fresh corn from the garden. She naively asked for butter, and the master gardeners present were aghast. "You don't ruin good sweet corn with butter," they sniffed.

Corn is a snap to make in the microwave, and because it doesn't get overcooked (or overboiled, I should say), it always comes out delicious.

I don't bother to remove the husks and silk. I simply check the tips, wrap the husks in plastic wrap, arrange it spoke fashion, and cook. See page 126.

If you choose to remove the silk and husk, wrap the corn in wax paper or put it in a dish. Take 1 minute off cooking times for each ear. The following chart is a guide.

Cook on High

1 ear:	2–3 minutes	let stand 3 or 4 minutes
2 ears:	5–6 minutes	let stand 3 or 4 minutes
3 ears:	7–8 minutes	let stand 3 or 4 minutes
4 ears:	10–12 minutes	let stand 3 or 4 minutes
6 ears:	14–16 minutes	let stand 3 or 4 minutes

You may let the corn stand longer, if it suits your cooking schedule better. To open, slit the plastic wrap and husk lengthwise and snip off the end. The plastic and husk will then pull off together very easily. Be careful of the hot steam that may come too.

For one serving: Carbohydrate, grams 14
Calories 68   Protein, grams 2
Total fat, grams 0.5   Sodium, mg 3
Saturated fat, grams .07   Cholesterol, mg 0

WHAT'S-HER-NAME'S BAKED BEANS

SERVES 6

I'll tell you how these beans got their name, but it isn't a pretty story. The first time I met my future mother-in-law, I hoped to make a favorable impression, as would any aspiring bride. (After all, I had cooked my heart out for two years in pursuit of Tex.) I was all dolled up for the party we were to attend. She was really impressed with me—for the first hour of the party she called me Nancy, and for the second hour, Carol. ("It's a good thing she lives in California," I hissed to myself during the longest party of my life.)

Yes, we did become good friends. And she is a great cook. This is her recipe, and we've eaten this dish for years and love it. The beans go well with hamburgers and any kind of barbecued meat. The longer, slower cooking time helps to blend the flavors. As much as you might like to, don't eat the entire dish yourself. They are higher in sodium and fat than some bean dishes. But I can't resist just eating a few. As healthy as beans are for us, I think you should try a few too.

I have named it in her honor.

1	cup yellow onion, chopped
½	cup green pepper, chopped
1½	teaspoons dry mustard
½	teaspoon black pepper*
2	teaspoons dried oregano
2	tablespoons packed brown sugar
1	21-ounce can baked beans in tomato sauce

1. Put the onion and green pepper in a 2-quart covered casserole and cover. Cook on High for 2 or 3 minutes, stirring once during cooking. Drain and discard the liquid.

2. Add the dry mustard, black pepper, oregano, brown sugar, and beans, and mix well. Cover and cook on High 5 minutes, and stir. Cook on Medium (50 percent) 10 to 15 minutes. Stir well. Let stand covered 3 to 5 minutes.

---

*For "hotter" beans increase the black pepper to 1½ teaspoons. Freshly ground pepper has a better flavor.

For one serving:

Calories 144

Total fat, grams 1.3

Saturated fat, grams 0.4

Carbohydrate, grams 27

Protein, grams 6

Sodium, mg 441

Cholesterol, mg 7

MRS. RANEY'S WACKY CAKE—TV

SERVES 10

This recipe came from a friend, Penny Raney. I've adapted it to the microwave. The cake is sweet, moist, and delicious, in spite of the fact that it has no eggs and includes cider vinegar in its ingredients. Now that's wacky!

1	cup sugar
1½	cups cake flour
3	tablespoons cocoa
1	teaspoon baking soda
¼	teaspoon salt
⅓	cup vegetable oil
1	cup water
1	teaspoon pure vanilla extract
1	teaspoon cider vinegar
	Powdered sugar for garnish (optional)

1. Coat a 9-inch cake pan with vegetable-oil spray and line with wax paper. Set aside.

2. Sift the sugar, flour, cocoa, soda, and salt together in an 4- to 6-cup measure. Set aside. In another container of the same size, mix the oil, water, vanilla extract, and vinegar. Pour the liquid ingredients into the dry ingredients and mix well. Pour into the prepared cake pan.

3. Cook, uncovered, on Medium (50 percent) 6 minutes, then cook on High 2 to 4 minutes. Let stand, covered, 5 minutes. Allow the cake to cool 5 minutes, then remove it from the pan. Dust with powdered sugar.

For one serving:
Calories 211
Total fat, grams 7
Saturated fat, grams 1.8

Carbohydrate, grams 35
Protein, grams 2
Sodium, mg 156
Cholesterol, mg 0

Menu 12.

La Comida

Mexican Lime Chicken*

Mexican Green Rice*

Refried Beans (Refritos)*

Mixed Lettuces

Hot Flour Tortillas

Baked Flan* with Caramel Sauce

MEXICAN LIME CHICKEN

SERVES 4

- ½ cup fresh lime juice (about 2 limes)
- ½ cup water
- 2 cloves garlic, minced
- ½ cup cilantro, chopped stems and leaves
- 4 chicken breast halves, skinned (about 2 pounds)
  Fresh cilantro leaves for garnish
  Slices of fresh lime for garnish

1. Mix together the lime juice, water, garlic, and cilantro in a 12″ × 8″ × 2″ flat dish. Add the chicken, cover, and marinate 2 to 3 hours in the refrigerator, turning the chicken several times.

2. Drain the marinade from the dish and arrange the chicken on a utility rack or (on a trivet in a 12″ × 8″ × 2″ baking dish) with the meatier portions to the outside. Cover with wax paper and cook on High 14 to 16 minutes, or until the juices run clear and the chicken is not pink. Let stand 4 minutes, covered. Garnish with cilantro and lime slices.

For one serving:
Calories 172
Total fat, grams 4
Saturated fat, grams 1.2

Carbohydrate, grams 3
Protein, grams 31
Sodium, mg 71
Cholesterol, mg 82

MEXICAN GREEN RICE

SERVES 4

This rice dish is a Wendy/Susan recipe. The rice is as delicious cold as it is hot.

Don't forget that beans and rice served together, called protein complements, add up to a nutritious meal higher in protein than either beans or rice served separately. Add just a small amount of animal protein from meat, milk, or cheese, and the protein levels go even higher.

Much of the world eats combinations of beans, grains, nuts, and seeds together to fill most of their protein needs, and rely on meat only occasionally. Because beans, grains, nuts, and seeds are also high in complex carbohydrates, they should be included in your diet.

1   medium white onion, chopped
1   clove garlic, minced
1   teaspoon olive oil
1   cup fresh parsley, minced
1   4-ounce can green chilies, diced and undrained
2   cups low-fat chicken stock, homemade (or broth, bouillon, or consommé)
    Salt to taste
1   cup long-grain converted rice

1. Put the onion, garlic, and oil in a 2-quart container, and cover. Cook on High for 2 or 3 minutes. Add the parsley, chilies, stock, salt, and rice.

2. Cook, uncovered, on High 20 minutes, or until rice has absorbed most of the stock. Let stand, covered, for 5 minutes.

TIP: For a spicier dish, substitute an equal amount of Rotel diced tomatoes with green chilies for the diced green chilies.

For one serving:
Calories 175
Total fat, grams 1.7
Saturated fat, grams 0.3

Carbohydrate, grams 34
Protein, grams 5
Sodium, mg 218
Cholesterol, mg 0

REFRIED BEANS (REFRITOS)

SERVES 4

Of course, you could make an entire meal with just Refried Beans and the Mexican Green Rice. The beans are simple and delicious as printed here, and a perfect accompaniment to the chicken. For a different treat, you could also garnish the beans with a dollop of yogurt, fresh cilantro leaves, and canned sliced jalapeño peppers.

    1   16-ounce can pinto beans, drained and rinsed
   1½   teaspoons olive oil
    ½   cup white onions, chopped
    ½   teaspoon garlic powder
        Salsa for garnish
        Canned jalapeño peppers, sliced, for garnish

1. Process the beans in a food processor or mash them with a potato masher. Set aside.

2. In a 1-quart casserole, stir together the oil, onion, and garlic powder, and cover. Cook on High for 2 to 3 minutes, or until onions are soft. Add the beans.

3. Cook, uncovered, on High 5 minutes, or until the beans are dry. Garnish with salsa and jalapeños, if you wish.

For one serving:	Carbohydrate, grams 19
Calories 110	Protein, grams 6
Total fat, grams 1.1	Sodium, mg 375
Saturated fat, grams 0.18	Cholesterol, mg 0

TIP—TO HEAT FLOUR TORTILLAS: As many as a dozen tortillas can be softened at one time. The heating time will depend on the freshness of the tortillas. If yours are old, spritz them with water and add a few seconds to the heating time.

Wrap 3 to 5 tortillas together in a microwave paper towel. A rubber band will hold the bundle together nicely. Cook on High 6 to 10 *seconds*. For 12 tortillas, cook on High 30 to 45 seconds, or until hot.

BAKED FLAN WITH CARAMEL SAUCE

SERVES 4

I won't say that the microwave was invented just to cook custard, but I have certainly thought it. Custard is so effortless to make in the microwave that you will probably never want to stand over a double boiler and stir custard again! And custard comes out perfect every time, with no scorching or curdled bits of egg, as can happen with the traditional cooking approach.

The lower cooking power will keep the eggs from curdling and won't toughen the egg protein. The custard will be pale if you use egg whites, so you might want to add a few drops of yellow food coloring.

Just as it is important for all foods to cook uniformly, custard is no different. I suggest that you rearrange the cups a time or two during cooking to ensure that they are cooked evenly.

1 cup egg whites* (about 8 egg whites or 1 cup egg substitute)
3 tablespoons sugar
1 teaspoon pure vanilla extract
1 cup skim milk
  Dashes of nutmeg, freshly grated is best
  Several drops yellow food coloring (optional)*
4 tablespoons commercial caramel sauce

1. In a 1-quart container, combine the egg whites, sugar, and vanilla extract. Whisk together until well blended and the sugar is dissolved.

2. Put the milk in a 2-cup measure. Cook on High 1½ to 2 minutes, or until very hot, but not to boiling (190 degrees F). Stir the milk into the egg mixture, a tablespoon at a time, so the eggs won't curdle.

3. Pour the mixture into 4 individual custard cups and sprinkle each with nutmeg. Place the cups in a circle on a flat tray or dish for easy handling. Cook, uncovered, on Medium (50 percent) 5 to 8 minutes, until slightly set. Rearrange several times. Cool, slightly uncovered, then chill before serving.

4. To serve, remove the flans from the containers and place each on a plate. Spoon 1 tablespoon of caramel sauce on top of each flan or on the plate around the flan. Sprinkle the top with additional nutmeg.

*If using egg whites, add a dash or 2 of yellow food coloring. Otherwise the flan will be very pale.

For one serving:
Calories 168
Total fat, grams 1.7
Saturated fat, grams 1

Carbohydrate, grams 29
Protein, grams 9
Sodium, mg 150
Cholesterol, mg 6

Menu 13.

Easy Buffet for Eight

Roast Pork with Honey Mustard Glaze*

Curried Fruit*

Fresh Vegetable Medley—TV*

Crab and Rice Romanoff*

"Dilly" Potato Salad*

Cherry-Chocolate Upside-down Cake—TV*

Georgia Peach Cheesecake*

ROAST PORK WITH HONEY MUSTARD GLAZE

SERVES 8

No matter how much I love my microwave for saving my heart and making my life simpler in general, meat and poultry grilled out-of-doors are hard to beat. Besides, we all know that men *love to cook outdoors, so this is one of those times you can get* him *to do a major part of the cooking while you sit around being charming.*

These days pork is a much leaner meat than it was in years past. Choose loin cuts for the lowest fat content.

Roast Pork with Honey Mustard Glaze uses the advantages of both the microwave and the grill. The real *reason I like to cook using both methods is that plenty of fat is extracted from the meat. By using the microwave and the grill, your meat will be juicier than if you simply grilled it. Also, using both methods shortens the time we have to "fiddle" over the hot grill—remember, most of us do our outdoor cooking when it is hot outside.*

You may use a commercial honey mustard or use the following recipe to make your own.

Much of the buffet can be prepared ahead of time. The Curried Fruit, "Dilly" Potato Salad, Chocolate Cake, Cheese Cake, Mustard Glaze for the Pork Roast, and Crab Romanoff are all dishes to prepare in advance.

For the pork, complete the microwave portion of the cooking instructions before your guests arrive, and put the roast on the grill as they walk in the door. The Crab Romanoff and Curried Fruit can be reheated and the Vegetable Medley can be cooked just before serving. Now, relax and enjoy your guests.

Bon appétit!

¼   cup honey
2   tablespoons freshly grated orange peel
¼   cup fresh orange juice
¼   cup country-style or coarse ground mustard
¼   teaspoon ground ginger
    Salt to taste
¼   teaspoon red or cayenne pepper
1   3- to 4-pound pork loin roast, boneless and tied

1. Combine the honey, orange peel, orange juice, mustard, ginger, salt, and red pepper in a 2-cup measure and mix thoroughly. Cook on high for 1 minute. Set aside.

2. Place the pork roast, fat side down, on a utility rack. Cover with wax paper. Cook on Medium (50 percent) for 7 minutes per pound. Turn the meat over after half the cooking time.

3. Meanwhile, prepare the outdoor grill. Place the wire rack 4 to 6 inches over the drip pan, and place the partially cooked roast on the rack. Cover the grill and open the vents slightly.

4. Cook the roast 35 to 40 minutes, turning it over after half the cooking time. Brush with the honey mustard sauce every 10 minutes throughout the grilling time. The meat will be ready to remove from the grill when

a meat thermometer registers a uniform 155 degrees F in several parts of the roast.

5. Place the roast on a carving board. Cover it with foil, shiny-side down, for about 10 minutes. The internal temperature will rise about 5 more degrees to the serving temperature of 160 degrees F. Carve the meat across the grain into thin slices.

TIP: Leftover pork can be combined in other delicious dishes or made into sandwiches. The leftover roast freezes well.

TIP: In case of grill "flare-ups," have a spritzer bottle with water handy.

For one serving:		Carbohydrate, grams 2
Calories 210	—	Protein, grams 28
Total fat, grams 10		Sodium, mg 192
Saturated fat, grams 3		Cholesterol, mg 85

CURRIED FRUIT

SERVES 8

Tex grew up eating a variation of Curried Fruit, another of his mother's recipes. (That woman can only cook tasty food!) Use unsweetened fruits or fruits packed in their own juice for fewer calories.

1   cup fresh grapes
1   8-ounce can pineapple chunks, drained
1   8-ounce can sliced peaches, drained
1   8-ounce can apricots, drained
1   8-ounce can fruit cocktail, drained
2   tablespoons unsalted vegetable-oil margarine

¼ cup packed brown sugar
½ teaspoon fresh lemon juice
¼ teaspoon cinnamon
1   teaspoon curry powder

1. Arrange the fruits in layers in a 1½ or 2-quart glass baking dish in the following order: grapes, pineapple, peaches, apricots, and fruit cocktail.

2. Put the margarine in a 1-cup measure. Cook on Medium (50 percent) for 1 to 1½ minutes. Add the brown sugar, lemon juice, cinnamon, and curry powder. Mix well, pour over the fruit, and cover.

3. Cook 4 minutes on High, stirring after 2 minutes. Let stand, covered, for 5 minutes. Serve warm.

TIP: Curry powder can stain microwave plastics. For this recipe, I use a clear glass baking dish.

For one serving: Carbohydrate, grams 23
Calories 121   Protein, grams 0.7
Total fat, grams 3   Sodium, mg 6
Saturated fat, grams 0.6 Cholesterol, mg 0

FRESH VEGETABLE MEDLEY—TV

SERVES 8

You may select your own mix of colorful and fresh vegetables. I've included carrots, broccoli, cauliflower, yellow crookneck and zucchini squash, and red bell pepper because they are my favorites.
This attractive fresh-vegetable presentation is always a cooking-class and TV favorite.

    1   cup carrots, cut in coins
   1½   cups broccoli flowerets
   1½   cups cauliflowerets
    ½   medium yellow squash, sliced
    ½   medium zucchini squash, sliced
    ½   red bell pepper, cut in rings

1. Place a plastic trivet in the bottom of an 8- to 10-inch flat glass plate. Arrange the "hardest" vegetables, such as carrots, on the outer edge of the plate. Next, alternate broccoli and cauliflower around the carrots. Arrange the more tender vegetables, such as squash, in the center of the plate. Place the peppers on top and cover completely with wax paper.

2. Cook on High for 10 to 16 minutes, or 5 to 7 minutes per pound. Let stand 2 minutes.

For one serving: Carbohydrate, grams 5
Calories 28   Protein, grams 2
Total fat, grams 0.2   Sodium, mg 18
Saturated fat, grams 0.04   Cholesterol, mg 0

CRAB AND RICE ROMANOFF

SERVES 8

    4   cups hot cooked rice* (page 295)
    ¼   cup fresh chives, chopped
    1   cup low-fat cottage cheese, small curd
    1   8-ounce can mushroom buttons, drained and rinsed
    ½   cup nonfat yogurt

*If you wish to use frozen or chilled rice, simply reheat before adding to the recipe. Each cup of rice reheats in about 1 to 1½ minutes on High.

 ½   cup reduced-calorie mayonnaise
 ¼   teaspoon white pepper
1½   teaspoons Worcestershire sauce
 ¼   cup Parmesan cheese
 2   7½-ounce cans lump crabmeat, rinsed and drained
        (or 2 cups fresh crabmeat)
      Paprika for garnish

1. In a large bowl, combine the rice, chives, cottage cheese, and mushrooms. Set aside.

2. In a separate bowl, blend the yogurt, mayonnaise, pepper, Worcestershire sauce, and 2 tablespoons of the cheese and fold into the rice mixture. Add the crabmeat, taking care not to break apart the lumps.

3. Spoon the mixture into a shallow 2-quart baking dish and sprinkle with the remaining cheese. Cook on Medium High (70 percent) for 6 to 8 minutes, or until the mixture is thoroughly heated. Garnish with paprika.

For one serving: Carbohydrate, grams 28
Calories 210   Protein, grams 17
Total fat, grams 3.3   Sodium, mg 463
Saturated fat, grams 0.8   Cholesterol, mg 57

"DILLY" POTATO SALAD

SERVES 8

1½   pounds medium red potatoes
 1   tablespoon water
      Salt to taste
 ¼   teaspoon black (or white) pepper
 ¼   cup fresh dill (or 1 tablespoon dried)
 ¼   cup green onions, thinly sliced

¼   cup red bell pepper, chopped
2   tablespoons nonfat yogurt
2   tablespoons reduced-calorie mayonnaise
1   teaspoon Dijon mustard
1   tablespoon white wine
¼   teaspoon sugar
    Fresh dill sprigs for garnish

1. Scrub and cut the potatoes in 4 or 6 pieces. Place them in a 6- or 8-cup measure. Add the water and cover. Cook on High 8 to 9 minutes. Drain the liquid and let stand 5 minutes, covered.

2. While the potatoes are still warm, sprinkle them with the salt, pepper, dill, onions, and red bell pepper. Toss carefully.

3. In a 1-cup measure, mix the yogurt, mayonnaise, mustard, wine, and sugar. Pour the dressing over the warm potatoes and mix. Let stand 10 minutes, then refrigerate. Garnish with sprigs of fresh dill.

For one serving: Carbohydrate, grams 15
Calories 74   Protein, grams 2
Total fat, grams 0.6   Sodium, mg 37
Saturated fat, grams 0.1   Cholesterol, mg .2

CHERRY-CHOCOLATE UPSIDE-DOWN CAKE—TV

SERVES 12

Serving this on a footed cake stand creates an elegant party atmosphere.

1   cup canned cherry-pie filling
¾   cup sugar

1½   cups cake flour
⅓   cup cocoa
1   teaspoon baking soda
½   teaspoon salt
½   teaspoon cinnamon
⅓   cup vegetable oil
¾   cup water
1   teaspoon pure vanilla extract
1   teaspoon cider vinegar

1. Coat an 8-cup ring or Bundt pan with vegetable-oil spray. Place three fourths of the cherry-pie filling in the bottom of the pan. Set aside.

2. In a large mixing bowl, sift together the sugar, flour, cocoa, baking soda, salt, and cinnamon.

3. In another bowl, combine the oil, water, vanilla extract, and vinegar. Pour the liquid ingredients into the dry ingredients and blend with an electric mixer for 1½ minutes on Medium speed. Add the remaining cherry-pie filling. Blend 30 seconds.

4. Pour the batter evenly into the cake mold. Cook, uncovered, on Medium (50 percent) 8 minutes, then cook on High for 2 to 6 minutes. Let the cake stand, covered, 10 minutes, until moist areas have disappeared. Remove the cake from the pan, cherry side up.

TIP: If you don't have a ring or Bundt pan, place an inverted custard cup in the center of a round 2-quart baking dish.

For one serving: Carbohydrate, grams 29
Calories 177   Protein, grams 2
Total fat, grams 5.9   Sodium, mg 95
Saturated fat, grams 1.6   Cholesterol, mg 0

GEORGIA PEACH CHEESECAKE

SERVES 8

1 graham-cracker crust (made without cinnamon), (see page 186)
3 egg whites
¾ cup granulated sugar
1½ teaspoons pure vanilla extract
8 ounces nonfat yogurt cheese, softened (see page 333)
8 ounces Neufchatel cheese (or light cream cheese) softened
½ cup light sour cream
2 teaspoons powdered sugar
¼ teaspoon pure vanilla extract
2 fresh peaches, peeled, sliced, and tossed with 1 teaspoon sugar

1. In a large bowl, beat the egg whites until they are stiff. Add the granulated sugar gradually and continue beating. Add the vanilla extract and the two cheeses. Continue beating with an electric mixer on High speed until creamy and smooth (about 3 minutes).

2. Pour the mixture into a *cooled* crust. Cook uncovered on Medium (50 percent) for 14 to 17 minutes, or until the center is almost set. Chill for 3 or more hours.

3. Meanwhile, place the sour cream, the 2 teaspoons powdered sugar and the ¼-teaspoon vanilla extract together in a small mixing bowl and blend thoroughly.

4. After the cheesecake has chilled, spread the topping over the cheesecake. Garnish each serving with 2 or 3 peach slices.

TIP—FOR HIGHER-VOLUME EGG WHITES: Room-temperature egg whites produce a higher volume. Remove the eggs
from the refrigerator about 30 minutes before beating them.

Use a copper or stainless-steel bowl for beating egg
whites. (A plastic bowl will "hold" fats from prior foods
and decrease the volume of your egg whites.)

For one serving: Carbohydrate, grams 36
Calories 279   Protein, grams 8
Total fat, grams 12   Sodium, mg 229
Saturated fat, grams 7   Cholesterol, mg 27

Menu 14.

Susan's Favorite Summer Dinner

Mediterranean Supper* over Bulgur

Green Salad

Low-Fat Frozen Yogurt

MEDITERRANEAN SUPPER

SERVES 6

Mediterranean Supper is delicious served over brown rice, one of my favorite standbys. But bulgur, if you haven't tried it, is nutty, flavorful, and wonderful with this dish too. Besides, it is Mediterranean—Turkish to be exact. Bulgur is simply whole-wheat kernels that have been cooked, toasted, and cracked—the whole-food equivalent to instant rice, but a lot better for you. And since bulgur is so healthy and can be cooked in mere minutes, you should make it a mainstay in your diet. It is available in many grocery stores in the produce section, or at health-food stores.

And what is Susan's favorite way to round out this meal? A green salad, of course, and then, go out for nonfat frozen yogurt. You knew I would slip it in somewhere, didn't you?

This is just as good as a leftover as it is fresh.

2½ cups cooked bulgur (or brown rice)
1 cup yellow onion, chopped
½ cup green pepper, chopped
2 teaspoons olive oil
2 cloves garlic, minced
1½ cups zucchini squash, coarsely chopped
1 cup fresh tomatoes, coarsely chopped

1   tablespoon fresh tarragon, chopped (or 1 teaspoon
        dried)
1   teaspoon dried oregano leaves
2   tablespoons fresh basil, chopped (or 2 teaspoons
        dried)
    Salt to taste
½   teaspoon black pepper
1   16-ounce can black beans, rinsed and drained
    Nonfat yogurt for garnish (optional)

1. Boil 3 cups of hot water. Place the bulgur in a 6-cup
   measure. Stir in the water, cover and set aside for 5 to
   10 minutes or until all the water is absorbed.

2. In a 3-quart casserole, combine the onions, green pepper, oil, and garlic, and cover. Cook on High 3 to 5
   minutes or until the vegetables are soft.

3. Add the squash, tomatoes, tarragon, oregano, basil, salt,
   and pepper, stir, and cover. Cook on High 4 minutes.

4. Add the beans, stir, and cover. Cook on High 4 to 6
   minutes or until heated thoroughly. Let stand 2 minutes. Serve over the hot bulgur and garnish with a dollop of yogurt.

For one serving: Carbohydrate, grams 21
Calories 122   Protein, grams 6.5
Total fat, grams 2   Sodium, mg 188
Saturated fat, grams 0.3 Cholesterol, mg 0

Menu 15.

Picnic in the Park

Spicy Chicken—TV*

Our Favorite "New" Potato Salad—TV*

Green Beans with Vidalia Onions*

Not-So-Sinful Brownies—TV*

SPICY CHICKEN—TV

SERVES 4

Spicy Chicken was a favorite TV recipe.

   2 tablespoons Dijon mustard
   2 tablespoons reduced-calorie mayonnaise
   ½ teaspoon cayenne pepper
   ¼ teaspoon black pepper
      Salt to taste
   ½ cup cornflake crumbs
   4 chicken breast halves, skinned (about 2 pounds)

1. Combine the mustard, mayonnaise, and seasonings in a small bowl. Set aside.

2. Put the cornflake crumbs in a shallow dish. Brush the chicken with the mayonnaise/mustard mixture, then coat it with the cornflakes. Place the chicken on a utility rack, putting the meatier portion to the outside. Cover with wax paper.

3. Cook on High for 8 to 10 minutes per pound (4 to 5 minutes per piece). Let stand 5 minutes, covered loosely with wax paper.

TIP: Try toasted wheat germ instead of the crushed cornflakes.

For one serving:	Carbohydrate, grams 6
Calories 205	Protein, grams 34
Total fat, grams 5	Sodium, mg 178
Saturated fat, grams 1.4	Cholesterol, mg 82

OUR FAVORITE "NEW" POTATO SALAD—TV

SERVES 4

This recipe has become a staple at our house. We serve it over lettuce as a salad, or by itself with any kind of sandwich or barbecued meat. It contains no mayonnaise, which makes it a picnic favorite.

1	pound new red potatoes, about golf-ball size, unpeeled
1	tablespoon water
1	tablespoon olive oil
1	tablespoon red wine vinegar
1	teaspoon Dijon mustard, country-style
1	teaspoon fresh marjoram (or 1 teaspoon dried)
	Salt to taste
⅛	teaspoon white pepper
2	tablespoons green onions (about 1 onion), thinly sliced
2	tablespoons fresh parsley, chopped

1. Scrub and cut the potatoes into ¼-inch slices or quarters. Place the potatoes in a 4- to 6-cup measure. Add water and cover. Cook on High 6 to 7 minutes. Drain all the liquid and let stand 5 minutes, covered.

2. In a 1-cup measure, mix together the oil, vinegar, mustard, marjoram, salt, and pepper. Pour the mixture over the potatoes while they are still warm. Mix carefully,

so as not to break the potatoes apart, then add the green onions and parsley. Chill before serving.

For one serving:
Calories 151
Total fat, grams 2.5
Saturated fat, grams 0.5

Carbohydrate, grams 29
Protein, grams 3
Sodium, mg 28
Cholesterol, mg 0

GREEN BEANS AND VIDALIA ONIONS

SERVES 4

I grew up eating "country" green beans that had been cooked about three days with bacon drippings or ham hock. I have never liked any other green beans as long as I have lived. This simple recipe is the only one I have tried that I can honestly say tastes good enough to fool with, if you can't have the good old-fashioned ones.

Georgia is famous for her sweet Vidalia onions, and they make this dish extra special. Other sweet onions are grown—Texas "Sweets" or Maui onions from Hawaii, for example. You will discover other sweet onions in your market, so give them a try. If sweet onions are out of season, substitute a yellow onion.

Green Beans with Vidalia Onions is the recipe that convinced my husband of many years that I had been hiding my talent for cooking. His reaction to this dish was "Why, these are good, I didn't know you had it in you." Apparently, he didn't remember the "early days," when I was chasing him with chocolate-chip cookies in one hand and shrimp cocktail in the other!

4   cups fresh green beans (about 1 pound)
1   medium Vidalia (or other sweet onion), sliced and
    separated into rings
1   cup low-fat chicken stock, homemade (or broth,
    bouillon, or consommé)
½   teaspoon salt (optional)

1. Snip off the ends of the green beans and cut them in 1½- to 2-inch pieces. Set aside.

2. Place the onion and chicken stock into a 1½-quart container and cover. Cook on High 3 minutes. Stir in (optional) salt to dissolve. Add the green beans.

3. Cook on High 15 to 18 minutes, stirring 2 or 3 times. Let stand 4 to 5 minutes.

TIP: Squeeze a lemon wedge or 2 over the beans for a different flavor.

For one serving:	Carbohydrate, grams 12
Calories 66	Protein, grams 3
Total fat, grams 0.7	Sodium, mg 17
Saturated fat, grams 0.16	Cholesterol, mg 0

NOT-SO-SINFUL BROWNIES—TV

MAKES 16 SQUARES

A favorite TV recipe. Friends and neighbors have had to "suffer" through all eight versions of these brownies, as I tried to get them just right for you. Funny, no one ever complained.

¼   cup unsalted vegetable-oil margarine
2   egg whites (or 2 ounces egg substitute)

¾   cup cake flour
1   teaspoon pure vanilla extract
5   tablespoons cocoa
⅔   cup sugar
½   teaspoon baking powder
     Chopped walnuts or pecans for garnish (optional)

1. Coat an 8″ × 8″ × 2″ baking dish with vegetable-oil spray. Set aside.

2. Put the margarine in 4- to 6-cup measure. To melt, cook on Medium (50 percent) 1 to 2 minutes. Add the egg whites, flour, vanilla, cocoa, sugar, and baking powder, and mix just until blended. Spoon evenly into a baking dish and sprinkle with nuts. Shield the corners of the dish with foil, but don't let the foil touch the sides of the microwave (see page 117 on shielding).

3. Cook, uncovered, on Medium High (70 percent) for 1 minute. Remove the foil. Cook on High for 2 to 3 minutes, or until the top springs back when touched. Let stand, covered, 5 minutes. Cool, then cut.

For one serving: Carbohydrate, grams 13
Calories 84   Protein, grams 1
Total fat, grams 3   Sodium, mg 16
Saturated fat, grams 0.65   Cholesterol, mg 0

Menu 16.

Sunday Night Supper

Tom Sinkovitz Red-Hot Chili—TV*

Green Salad

Peppery Corn Muffins—TV*

Banana Pudding Almost Like "Mama"
Used to Make—TV*

TOM SINKOVITZ RED-HOT CHILI—TV

SERVES 6

On the night before one of my Atlanta TV segments, I was watching the evening news, when what did I hear but a "tease" for my cooking segment the next day.

"Tomorrow, our microwave whiz, Susan Nicholson, will prepare a dish for us that is so hot she's named it after our reporter Tom Sinkovitz."

Oh no. Now what am I going to say when they ask me why I named the dish after Tom? First of all, it had turkey in it. I couldn't say the turkey reminded me of Tom—not if I wanted to live through it, and besides, he's a nice guy.

I knew he was single (then)—how about that for hot? But how would I know he was hot? Oh, jeez. That wouldn't work. I didn't get a wink of sleep that night. I figured my career was over.

The show went well. Tom came on the segment and was a good sport about the whole thing. He helped stir the chili and never asked why I named it after him. But every time I think about it and eat the chili, I feel like a turkey.

This chili is even better the next day.

1½   cups white onion, chopped
  1   pound ground turkey (or ground round)

1   clove garlic, minced
1   6-ounce can tomato paste, no salt added
1   10-ounce can Rotel diced tomatoes with green
      chilies
1   30-ounce can chili beans with liquid
1   tablespoon chili powder
    Salt to taste
1   tablespoon cumin
2   tablespoons balsamic vinegar
¼   cup green onions, chopped for garnish (optional)
    Nonfat yogurt for garnish (optional)

1. Place the onion in a colander over a 3-quart container and cover. Cook on High 2 minutes. Add the turkey (or beef) and garlic. Cook on High 5 to 6 minutes, or until the meat is no longer pink. Stir several times, breaking the meat apart. Discard the grease and liquid that has collected in the bottom container.

2. Put the cooked meat/onion mixture in the bottom container. Add the tomato paste, tomatoes with green chilies, beans and liquid, chili powder, salt, and cumin, and cover. Cook on High 5 minutes. Then cook on Low (30 percent) for 20 to 30 minutes, stirring several times.

3. Stir in the balsamic vinegar and let stand, covered, 5 minutes.

4. Garnish with optional onions and nonfat yogurt.

TIP: If you aren't familiar with Rotel (brand name) Mexican-style tomatoes, now is a good time to learn—they are a spicy addition to many dishes that need extra zing. Look for them in the grocery store near the canned tomatoes.

For one serving: Carbohydrate, grams 34
Calories 280   Protein, grams 27

Total fat, grams 4   Sodium, mg 750
Saturated fat, grams 1   Cholestrol, mg 42

PEPPERY CORN MUFFINS

MAKES 8 MUFFINS

Don't forget that the double layer of paper liners in your muffin pan helps absorb moisture and gives muffins a better texture.

½   cup frozen whole-kernel corn
½   cup cake flour
⅓   cup red bell pepper, chopped
¼   teaspoon cumin
¼   teaspoon chili powder
2   egg whites (or ¼ cup egg substitute)
½   cup yellow cornmeal
2   teaspoons baking powder
⅓   cup skim milk
2   tablespoons vegetable oil

1. Put 2 papers in each cup of a muffin pan or custard cups.*

2. Put the corn in a a-cup measure and cover. Cook on High 2 minutes. Drain thoroughly.

3. Combine the corn, flour, bell pepper, cumin, chili powder, egg whites, cornmeal, baking powder, milk, and oil in a small mixing bowl and stir until just blended.

*If you are using custard cups, arrange them in a circle in the micro-wave.

4. Fill the muffin cups about half full. Cook, uncovered, on High for 2 to 3 minutes for 6 muffins or 20 to 30 seconds for 1, or until the muffin tops spring back when touched. Let stand 1 to 2 minutes.

TIP: If you use canned corn, drain and rinse thoroughly. Canned corn is higher in sodium.

For one serving: Carbohydrate, grams 14
Calories 104   Protein, grams 3
Total fat, grams 4   Sodium, mg 124
Saturated fat, grams 0.9 Cholesterol, mg 0

BANANA PUDDING ALMOST LIKE "MAMA" USED TO MAKE—TV

SERVES 6

This Banana Pudding is my most popular TV recipe of all time. If egg whites are used instead of egg substitute, the pudding will be very pale. A drop or two of yellow food coloring will improve the color.

When I make this pudding, Tex eats half of the recipe as a serving. He likes it.

2   tablespoons cornstarch
     Salt to taste
⅓   cup sugar
2   cups skim milk
⅓   cup egg whites (about 6 egg whites or ⅓ cup egg substitute)
1   teaspoon pure vanilla extract
1   teaspoon unsalted vegetable-oil margarine, melted
4   drops yellow food coloring (optional)
2   medium bananas
3   vanilla wafers, crumbled

1. Combine the cornstarch, salt, and sugar in a small mixing bowl and mix thoroughly.

2. Combine the milk, egg whites, vanilla, margarine, and food coloring in another 6-to 8-cup container. Whisk to blend. Add the dry ingredients and whisk all the ingredients together thoroughly and cover.

3. Cook on High 6 to 8 minutes, or until thick, stirring after every minute. To chill, place wax paper directly on the pudding, then refrigerate.

4. To assemble, slice the bananas on the bottom of a serving dish. Add the chilled banana pudding and garnish with crumbled vanilla wafers.

For one serving:
Calories 148
Total fat, grams 1.3
Saturated fat, grams 0.4

Carbohydrate, grams 27
Protein, grams 7
Sodium, mg 97
Cholesterol, mg 2

Menu 17.

Red Meat Treat

Swiss Steak*

Baked Potatoes*

Citrus Carrots*

Corn Muffins*

Good "Old-fashioned" Rice Pudding*

SWISS STEAK

SERVES 4

Almost everyone wants a dinner of beef once in a while, and what could be better than an easy Swiss Steak recipe? Just as in a conventional oven, less tender cuts of meat, such as the cubed steaks used below, have to be cooked for longer periods at low power to insure tender results. Using an acidic food such as tomatoes helps tenderize the meat.

But in the microwave the work is easier and faster. Of course, using a microwave doesn't heat your kitchen all day, and you don't have to check constantly for scorching or burning food.

    4   cubed steaks (4 or 5 ounces each)
    ¼   cup all-purpose flour
    1   15-ounce can stewed tomatoes, including liquid
    1   teaspoon Worcestershire sauce
    2   tablespoons fresh parsley, chopped

1. Pat the steaks dry. Coat both sides of the steaks in the flour and place them in a single layer in an 8″ × 12″ × 2″ flat baking dish.

2. Put the tomatoes in a mixing bowl and break them apart with a spoon. Add the Worcestershire sauce and parsley. Spoon the mixture over the steaks, making sure to cover them completely. Cover the container.

3. Cook on High for 3 minutes. Then cook on Medium (50 percent) for 5 minutes. Turn the steaks over and rearrange. Spoon the sauce over the steaks and cook on Medium (50 percent) 6 to 8 minutes, or until meat has lost its pink color. Let stand, covered, 3 to 5 minutes. (Thicker steaks will take a little longer.)

For one serving: Carbohydrate, grams 14
Calories 246   Protein, grams 33
Total fat, grams 6.4   Sodium, mg 384
Saturated fat, grams 2.2 Cholesterol, mg 83

BAKED POTATOES

SERVES 4

If you missed the instructions for baking potatoes in Chapter 5, I'll give you a review. Remember, microwaves cook by volume and density, so the more potatoes you cram in to the microwave, the longer they will take to cook. As needed, you can easily make more or fewer potatoes, and adjust the cooking time accordingly.

4 medium russet baking potatoes, about 6 to 8 ounces each

A timetable for cooking potatoes follows:

1 potato	3½ to 4½ minutes
2 potatoes	7 to 9 minutes
3 potatoes	10 to 12 minutes
4 potatoes	14 to 16 minutes

1. Scrub the potatoes and pierce them with a fork several times to prevent bursting. Place them on a paper towel

on a trivet. If you are cooking more than 1 or 2 potatoes, arrange them in spoke fashion.

2. Cook on High 3½ to 4½ minutes per potato, or about
   8 minutes per pound.

3. Wrap the potatoes in a paper-towel bundle, and then
   in a terry-cloth towel. Let stand 5 minutes to complete
   cooking. The potatoes will stay hot 30 or 40 minutes
   wrapped this way.

TIP: Cooking times for potatoes vary because of their
moisture content and age. Older, drier potatoes may not
bake as fast or as well.

For one serving:	
Calories 223	Carbohydrate, grams 51
Total fat, grams 0.2	Protein, grams 5
Saturated fat, grams 0.1	Sodium, mg 16
	Cholesterol, mg 0

CITRUS CARROTS

SERVES 4

*One of the benefits of becoming a "grown-up" is
never having to eat carrots again. Of course, I know
all about the nutritional value of carrots, and dearly
love them tucked into cakes. But cooked carrots?
Never.*

*I can still remember the Sunday dinners of my
childhood when we regularly dined on roast beef
with potatoes, carrots, and onions. My mother
would have the combination dinner ready to go in
the oven to start the cooking as we walked in the
door from Sunday morning church. (My father's*

standing rule at our house was Never leave the house with the oven turned on.*)*

My brother, Fritz, had a great trick he used to play on my mother. He did it so often that I thought she would surely catch on—after all, I was only six or seven years old, and I had figured it out. We would be sitting in church, which was next door to our house, and just before the music would begin, Fritz would whisper to my mother, "Mother, did you turn off the oven?" She would panic, fumble in her purse for the house key, and send him home to check the oven. Of course, he never returned to church.

Shifty little boy! Anyway, after church we would have to wait forever *for lunch. And finally, out would come the beef, potatoes, onions, and the* dreaded carrots. *I would feel faint just at the sight of them.*

My father told stories of how healthy carrots were, and that people who ate carrots could see better in the dark. Parents really know how to go on and on about such subjects. My reaction was to methodically take each carrot on my plate and wrap the "enemy" in a half-slice of bread, and swallow it whole. Gulp. (No wonder I was chubby.)

My feelings about carrots have not changed through the years. However, some *people like cooked carrots. The following recipe passed inspections by some of my carrot-loving friends. If you are one of* "those people," *you may enjoy them.*

If you don't like carrots, get your vitamin A someplace else. And remember, this dietitian told you, you don't have to eat your carrots!

2   cups carrots, peeled and sliced ¼"
1   tablespoon water
2   tablespoons fresh orange juice

½ teaspoon fresh orange zest*
1 teaspoon unsalted vegetable-oil margarine
¼ teaspoon ground ginger
¼ teaspoon pure vanilla extract
1 tablespoon fresh parsley, chopped

1. Combine the carrots, water, and orange juice in a 1-quart casserole, and cover. Cook on High 4½ to 6 minutes. Add the orange zest, margarine, ginger, and vanilla extract, and stir. Cover and let stand 3 minutes. Garnish with parsley.

For one serving: Carbohydrate, grams 9
Calories 50   Protein, grams 1
Total fat, grams 1.1   Sodium, mg 52
Saturated fat, grams 0.2 Cholesterol, mg 0

CORN MUFFINS

SERVES 6

½ cup cake flour
½ cup yellow cornmeal
2 teaspoons sugar
2 teaspoons baking powder
½ teaspoon salt (optional)
2 egg whites, slightly beaten
⅓ cup skim milk
2 tablespoons vegetable oil

1. Place 2 papers in each cup of a muffin pan or into custard cups.† Set aside.

*Cut off just the outer orange part of the peel, not the white part, which is bitter tasting.
†If you are using custard cups, arrange them in a circle in the microwave.

2. Sift together the flour, cornmeal, sugar, baking powder, and salt in a 6-cup measure. Add the egg whites, milk, and oil. Mix together until all ingredients are moistened.

3. Fill the muffin cups half full. Cook uncovered on High 1½ to 2½ minutes for 6 muffins or 15 to 25 seconds for 1, or until the muffins are almost dry on top. Let stand 3 minutes.

For one serving: 1 muffin   Carbohydrate, grams 18
Calories 131   Protein, grams 3.5
Total fat, grams 5   Sodium, mg 120
Saturated fat, grams 1.2   Cholesterol, mg 0

GOOD "OLD-FASHIONED" RICE PUDDING

SERVES 6

    2   cups skim milk
    ¼   cup long-grain converted rice
    2   tablespoons raisins
    2   teaspoons unsalted vegetable-oil margarine
    3   egg whites (or 3 ounces egg substitute), beaten
    2   tablespoons sugar
    ¼   teaspoon salt (optional)
    ⅛   teaspoon allspice
    ½   teaspoon pure vanilla extract
        Drops of yellow food coloring (optional)*

1. Combine the milk, rice, raisins, and margarine in a 6- to 8-cup measure. Cook uncovered, on High 4 to 5 minutes, or until steaming hot but not boiling (190 de-

---

*If using egg whites, add a dash or 2 of yellow food coloring to add color. Otherwise the pudding will be very pale.

grees F with your temperature probe or thermometer). Stir. Reduce power to Medium (50 percent) and cook, uncovered 20 to 25 minutes, stirring several times.

2. Combine the beaten egg whites, sugar, salt, and allspice in a 2-cup measure. Stir several tablespoons of the rice mixture into the egg mixture to equalize the temperature and prevent curdling.

3. Cook, uncovered, on Low (30 percent) 5 to 6 minutes, or until thickened. Stir in the vanilla extract. Let stand 3 minutes. Chill before serving.

For one serving:
Calories 96
Total fat, grams 1.4
Saturated fat, grams 0.3

Carbohydrate, grams 16
Protein, grams 5
Sodium, mg 67
Cholesterol, mg 1

On Flavor

I have heard criticisms that food cooked in the microwave does not have the depth of flavor as that of food cooked by traditional methods. But you can achieve the same depth of flavor in the microwave by using cooking principles you already know about—long, slow cooking. The Black Bean Soup that follows is especially delicious due to long, slow cooking on lower power.

The purpose of long, slow cooking is simple. The flavoring components in foods, whether chicken or celery or onions, are transferred into the liquid in which they are cooking. Then, if time allows, the flavors move back to the food. This exchange happens slowly. (That's why some foods like soups and stews taste better the next day).

Slow cooking allows starches to be turned to sugars, which gives many foods a sweeter flavor. Slow cooking also prevents the fluid loss and drier texture in some meats. Some foods are cooked more slowly on lower power for a more evenly cooked product—a large roasting hen, for example.

In the old days, microwave cooks cooked everything on *high* power. After all, speed was *all* we wanted from the microwave. No more. Now we know the microwave is good for so much more than speed—delicious food and healthier food.

Most people don't even think to *use* their microwaves for anything except *fast* cooking. I want *you* to help change that trend.

Menu 18.

Soup's On!

Mixed Green Salad

Black Bean Soup* with
Steamed Rice*

Beth's Vegetable Soup*

MMMMmm . . . Melting Peaches*

I have offered two soup recipes here, in case you want to have a "soup party," which is a wonderful way to entertain.

BLACK BEAN SOUP

MAKES 10 CUPS

This soup is delicious. I use canned black beans (also called turtle beans) because of the convenience. When you use canned beans as I have below, rinse them to remove any excess salt.

The flavor and body of the soup improves with "age"—each time you reheat it, it thickens and concentrates the flavor. It also freezes well.

1   clove garlic, minced
1   teaspoon olive oil
1   medium yellow onion, chopped
1   quart low-fat chicken stock, homemade (or broth, bouillon, or consommé)
1   16-ounce can stewed tomatoes, lightly drained
1   10-ounce can Rotel diced tomatoes with green chilies, lightly drained
3   16-ounce cans black beans, drained and rinsed
1   tablespoon fresh lemon juice
    Light sour cream (or nonfat yogurt) for garnish
    Paprika for garnish
    Sprigs of fresh cilantro for garnish

1. Put the garlic and oil in a 1-cup measure, and cover. Cook on High for 45 seconds. Set aside. Put the onions and chicken stock in a 3- or 4-quart container, and cover. Cook on High 8 to 10 minutes or until the onions are soft.

2. Add the garlic and oil to the onion/chicken-stock mixture. Cook on High 4 to 7 minutes, or until hot. Crush the tomatoes with a spoon. Add both kinds of tomatoes and the beans to the mixture, and cover. Cook on High 10 minutes. Stir and cook, uncovered, on High 15 minutes *or* cook on Low (30 percent) power for 30 to 45 minutes.

3. Place half the solids in the mixture in the work bowl of a food processor and puree slightly. Add the puree back to the soup to thicken it. Add the lemon juice and serve with a garnish of light sour cream or nonfat yogurt, a sprinkle of paprika, and a sprig of cilantro.

TIP: When I am in a hurry, sometimes I add 2 teaspoons of balsamic vinegar to deepen the flavor.

TIP: For a thicker soup, put ¼ cup cornstarch in a 2-cup measure. Using a whisk, stir in ¼ cup of water until the mixture is smooth.

Add several tablespoons of hot soup to the cornstarch to equalize the temperature. Add back to the soup and cook on High 5 minutes, or until the soup is as thick as you like.

For one serving:	Carbohydrate, grams 14
Calories 84	Protein, grams 4
Total fat, grams 1.1	Sodium, mg 280
Saturated fat, grams 0.2	Cholesterol, mg 0

STEAMED RICE

SERVES 4

Steamed rice can be used in so many ways—from rice pudding to pilafs to casseroles. Be careful not to stir the rice during cooking, for stirring will make it pasty. Remember that rice freezes well. I measure the leftovers into 1-cup quantities for the freezer.

You may substitute low-fat chicken stock for all or part of the liquid.

> 1   cup long-grain converted rice
> 2½   cups hot water
> 1   teaspoon salt (optional)

1. Combine the rice, water, and salt (optional) in a 3-quart casserole, and cover. (The rice is likely to boil over in a smaller container.) Cook on High 5 minutes, lower power to Medium (50 percent), and cook for 20 minutes. Let stand, covered, 5 minutes.

2. Fluff with a fork and serve. If the rice is too moist, cook on High, uncovered, for 1 to 2 additional minutes, or until the moisture is absorbed.

TIP: Two microwave paper towels placed under the rice will help catch any boilovers.

For one serving:	Carbohydrate, grams 37
Calories 167	Protein, grams 3
Total fat, grams 0.1	Sodium, mg 0
Saturated fat, grams 0	Cholesterol, mg 0

BETH'S VEGETABLE SOUP

MAKES 8 CUPS

Another Georgia transplant from Virginia, Beth Little shared her vegetable-soup recipe. I adapted her soup to the microwave and made a few "Beth approved" changes.

The first time we had this soup for dinner, Tex and his "wimpy" appetite polished off 4 cups (that's a quart, friends) of this hearty soup, along with crusty Italian bread spread with yogurt cheese and whatever the dessert for the day happened to be. That seemed to fill him sufficiently. Needless to say, he liked Beth's soup. (As our friends who invite us to dinner can attest, Tex can eat.)

1	teaspoon olive oil
1	clove garlic, minced
½	cup yellow onion, finely chopped
¼	cup carrots, finely chopped
½	cup celery without leaves, finely chopped
½	cup fresh mushrooms, sliced
1	cup frozen whole kernel corn, thawed and drained
1	cup cooked brown rice (or white rice)
1	15-ounce can garbanzo beans (chick-peas), rinsed and drained
2	cups tomato juice (or V-8), no salt added
3	cups low-fat chicken stock, homemade (or broth, bouillon, or consommé)
1	tablespoon fresh basil, chopped (or 1 teaspoon dried)
4	or 5 sprigs fresh thyme (or ½ teaspoon dried)
	Salt and pepper to taste

1. Put the oil, garlic, and onion in a 1-cup measure and cover. Cook on High 1½ to 2 minutes, or until the onions are soft.

2. Place the carrots, celery, mushrooms, and corn in a 3-quart container and cover. Cook on High 5 to 6 minutes, or until the vegetables are soft. Drain thoroughly.

3. To the carrot mixture add the onion mixture, cooked rice, beans, tomato juice, stock, and seasonings. Mix thoroughly and cover.

4. Cook on High 15 minutes. Stir and cook on Medium (50 percent) 20 to 30 minutes or Low (30 percent) for 40 to 50 minutes.

For one serving:	Carbohydrate, grams 29
Calories 158	Protein, grams 6
Total fat, grams 2	Sodium, mg 129
Saturated fat, grams 0	Cholesterol, mg 0

MMMMmm . . . MELTING PEACHES

SERVES 6

What a funny name for a recipe, you say. I named it for the reaction you will have when you taste these. Now could anything sooo simple be sooo delicious? Here's how:

4 cups peaches,* sliced (fresh if possible, or frozen and thawed)
1 tablespoon fresh lemon juice
½ teaspoon allspice
1 teaspoon pure vanilla extract
2 cups (white) miniature marshmallows

*If using canned peaches, drain them thoroughly.

1. Peel and slice the peaches* in a 1-quart casserole. Add the lemon juice and toss with the peaches to coat. Add the allspice and vanilla extract and mix thoroughly.

2. Cook, uncovered, on High 2 to 3 minutes. Top with the marshmallows. Cook, uncovered, on High 2 to 3 minutes, or until marshmallows are almost melted. Serve warm. MMMMMMMmmm.

TIP: To remove the skin from peaches, place peaches in the microwave on a microwave paper towel. For room-temperature peaches, cook on High 30 seconds for 1 peach. For chilled peaches, cook on High 1½ minutes for 1 peach. Let stand 10 minutes and remove the skin.

For one serving: Carbohydrate, grams 25
Calories 105   Protein, grams 1
Total fat, grams 0.1   Sodium, mg 6
Saturated fat, grams .01   Cholesterol, mg 0

*If using canned peaches, drain them thoroughly.

Menu 19.

Thanksgiving Feast

Brunswick Stew*

Baked Turkey—TV*

Apple Sage Dressing—TV*

Holiday Vegetable Ring—TV*

Baked Sweet Potatoes with Orange Zest*

Thanksgiving Gravy—TV*

Cranberry Sauce*

Pumpkin-Vanilla Pudding—TV*

TRADITIONS

For me, one memorable note about Thanksgiving is that I was born on that day. Because of my suspect choice of days, my parents and Dr. Love (isn't that great name for a birthing doctor?) missed the never-to-be-missed VMI/VPI (Virginia Military Institute/Virginia Polytechnic Institute) football game, as my arrival time in Harrisonburg and kickoff time in Roanoke coincided at 1:00 P.M. I was just in time for lunch, naturally.

The year I was born was the only year the family missed that ball game, which brings me to a discussion of the makings of our "proper" Thanksgiving meal. Tailgate food, not turkey, was our family's tradition.

The meal itself was prepared at the Whitmores', Burresses', and our kitchens. We ate on some church steps on the right-hand side of little Route 11, on the way to Roanoke and the traditional football game, or at the home of another Burress family in Roanoke. The proper meal consisted of country-ham and biscuit sandwiches, Brunswick stew, pimento cheese, brownies, and Virginia Gentleman (for the adults).

Now you know why I have such a peculiar reaction to turkey. Dressing? Cranberries? Never heard of them.

This story goes back to what I've said over and over; breaking a lifetime of habits is *not easy,* nor is creating new ones. I tell you my food stories over and over because I have struggled through some of the same struggles you have, in order to change the way I eat. Holidays have always been the hardest time for me to continue with my healthy eating.

Whether holidays are comfortable or uncomfortable times in your life, for most of us the foods we ate with the ones we loved gave comfort, if nothing else.

When I was a hospital dietitian, I gave my patients fire and brimstone to keep their diets in line. But when holidays rolled around, I would stretch diet therapy to the limit to give patients the traditional foods they craved.

You, too, can have the holiday foods you crave, without compromising your heart-healthy diet. The recipes below are all traditional favorites, and only one ingredient is missing: the fat.

So, enjoy Thanksgiving with Susan!

BRUNSWICK STEW

SERVES 8

If, for you, too, the traditional Thanksgiving dinner is too much, and you would prefer to have a buffet before or after the game, Brunswick Stew is the answer. If you show up at my house on Thanksgiving, this is what you will likely find us eating.

I took the recipe from a family friend who was one of my favorite grade school teachers, Frances Burress, and adapted it Save Your Heart–style. The results are great. Brunswick Stew is good any time of the year (as we know, here in the South). If you prepare it in the summer, fresh vegetables are wonderful (please refer to Chapter 9 for basic-vegetable cooking times). And leftovers can go in the freezer—after all, this recipe does make two quarts!

You may know by now that you can reduce the power level and increase the cooking time to help blend flavors. These tips might help you:

- Cook 20 minutes on Medium (50 percent) or 45 minutes on Low (30 percent) power.
- Cook without a lid to thicken the stew or add more chicken stock to thin it.

This recipe for Brunswick Stew reminds me of my mother. It was one of her favorites.

2	or 3 chicken breast halves, skinned (about 1 pound)
1	medium stalk celery without leaves, quartered
1	medium yellow onion, quartered
1	cup fresh parsley leaves, chopped in 2-inch pieces
2	cups low-fat chicken stock, homemade (or broth, bouillon, or consommé)
½	cup yellow onions, chopped
1	15-ounce can tomatoes, no salt added, chopped, with liquid
1	15-ounce can baby lima beans, rinsed and drained
2	cups frozen whole kernel corn, thawed
2	tablespoons sugar
½	teaspoon black pepper
¼	teaspoon red pepper
	Salt to taste
¼	cup dehydrated white potatoes*

1. Place the chicken breasts, celery, quartered onion, parsley, and chicken stock in a 3- or 4-quart container. Cook on High for 10 to 12 minutes or until juices are clear and the chicken is no longer pink. Remove the chicken from the stock and strain the stock. Discard the celery/parsley mixture. Set stock aside.

2. Put the chopped onion in a 1-cup measure and cook on High 1 minute. Drain the onions and set aside.

*You may use 1 whole potato, cooked, peeled, and mashed, if you prefer. A fresh potato is lower in sodium.

3. When the chicken is cool enough to touch, chop the meat into small pieces. To the chicken stock, stir in the chicken, chopped onions, tomatoes, lima beans, corn, sugar, black and red pepper, and salt to taste, and cover.

4. Cook on High 15 minutes, stirring halfway through the cooking time. (From now on, you may leave the dish covered for a thinner stew, or uncovered for a thicker stew.)

5. Stir in the dehydrated potatoes to thicken and cook on Medium (50 percent) for 10 minutes. Stir occasionally.

For one serving: Carbohydrate, grams 25
Calories 199 Protein, grams 18
Total fat, grams 3 Sodium, mg 212
Saturated fat, grams 0.9 Cholesterol, mg 34

BAKED TURKEY—TV

SERVES 6 WITH LEFTOVERS

Why use the microwave? The same reason we've been using it all along—it cooks poultry beautifully. Poultry cooked in the microwave is moist and oh, so juicy. Someday I will tell you about being a turkey farmerette in my youth, which is probably why I eat Brunswick Stew on Thanksgiving.

Buy a fresh turkey, not one that has been "injected" with "butter." A fresh turkey has a just-off-the-farm taste, and carries with it no extra injected (saturated) oils to muck up the progress you've made with saving your heart. You can also avoid those pop-up thermometers that tell you when the turkey is cooked—they don't work in the microwave.

Obviously, you need to buy a turkey that will fit in your microwave. An 8- to 12-pound turkey will probably be the upper size limit. Your microwave needs to be at least 1 cubic foot in size and have 600 to 700 watts. If yours doesn't, go out for lunch. (A turkey breast is an option if you have a smaller microwave.)

Yes, the microwave can defrost the turkey. I still prefer to defrost mine in the refrigerator for several days, and run cold water through it to finish defrosting, if necessary. Defrosting a turkey in the refrigerator is just one of those precautions I take with poultry.

The bird will require about 10 to 11 minutes a pound on High to cook. The size and shape of the bird will also determine cooking time: a broad-breasted bird will take longer to cook than one that is more streamlined. I don't "stuff" the turkey because the extra fat can soak into the dressing. Too, I am always concerned about the safety, and the high number of incidences of food poisoning.

I use a conventional oven cooking bag for my turkey. You know why—I'm lazy. It's the easiest way to cook the turkey evenly, and doesn't require that you turn the bird over four times for even cooking. When I tie the bag closed, I stick the handle of a wooden spoon in the bag opening, and close and tie the bag around it, then remove the spoon. The opening allows steam to escape and makes the bag easier to open for basting.

PS: Thanksgiving Dinner is a perfect time to use both of your microwaves!

Please remember these safety tips:

- *Thaw the turkey in the refrigerator or in cold water.*
- *Keep the turkey refrigerated until cooking time.*
- *Refrigerate all leftovers immediately.*
- *Finished internal turkey temperature is 185 to 190 F.*
- *Use the cooked turkey in 3 days for best results. Leftover turkey makes great sandwiches. The cooked meat will keep in the freezer for 3 months.*

Turkey Hot Line: Please refer to Appendix B for the telephone number for the Meat and Poultry Hot Line, a free hot-line service from the U.S. Department of Agriculture. They are even open on Thanksgiving Day!

1   **8- to 12-pound turkey, fresh or thawed**
¼   **cup unsalted vegetable-oil margarine**
    Browning agent—liquid or powder
½   **cup liquid (water, wine, or broth)**

1. Remove the giblets from the neck and cavity of the turkey.* Under cold running water, thoroughly wash the thawed turkey inside and out. Pat the turkey dry. Tie the legs together with string or a rubber band (not a "twisty"—they have metal in them). Fold some aluminum foil over the wings, drumsticks, and breastbone so they won't overcook.

---

*The heart, liver, gizzard, and neck of the turkey are usually packed together and collectively called the "giblets." To use the giblets for turkey stock, see the Thanksgiving Gravy recipe on page 310. I use the giblets for flavoring the stock but do not eat them, as they are very high in cholesterol.

2. Put the margarine in a 1-cup measure. To melt, cook on Medium (50 percent) for 2½ to 3½ minutes. Stir in the browning agent. Brush the margarine mixture all over the turkey.

3. Place the turkey in a conventional oven cooking bag, add the liquid, and tie the bag shut. Place the turkey on a trivet in a baking dish, slip the temperature probe or thermometer through the bag into the meatiest part of the inner thigh, without touching the bone.

4. Cook on High 10 to 11 minutes per pound. When turkey is half done, remove aluminum foil covering the wing tips, drumsticks, and breastbone. Baste with juices in the bag, close the bag, and continue to cook until the thermometer reads 180 degrees F in several places.

5. Remove the turkey from the bag and let stand for 20 minutes covered with a foil tent. The final temperature should read 185 degrees F. (Be sure to check the temperature in several places.)

For one serving:	Carbohydrate, grams 0
Calories 145	Protein, grams 25
Total fat, grams 4	Sodium, mg 63
Saturated fat, grams 1.4	Cholesterol, mg 65

APPLE-SAGE DRESSING—TV

SERVES 6

 2 tablespoons unsalted vegetable-oil margarine
 ⅓ cup celery without leaves, sliced
 ⅓ cup green onions, sliced
 4 cups unseasoned bread cubes, toasted
 ¼ teaspoon dried sage

½   cup red apple, unpeeled and chopped
¾   cup low-fat chicken (or turkey) stock, homemade (or
      broth, bouillon, or consommé)

1. Put the margarine in a 2-cup measure. To melt, cook
   on Medium (50 percent) for 30 seconds to 1 minute.
   Add the celery and onions and cover.

2. Cook on High for 2 to 2½ minutes, or until the vegetables are soft.

3. Mix together the bread cubes, sage, apple, and stock in
   a 2-quart casserole, and stir in the vegetable mixture.
   Cover and cook on High 3 to 5 minutes. Let stand 2
   minutes.

For one serving: Carbohydrate, grams 19
Calories 133   Protein, grams 3
Total fat, grams 5   Sodium, mg 183
Saturated fat, grams 1   Cholesterol, mg 1

HOLIDAY VEGETABLE RING—TV

SERVES 6

4   cups broccoli flowerets
4   cups cauliflowerets
1   tablespoon water
8   thin strips of yellow bell pepper
1   tablespoon unsalted vegetable-oil margarine
1   teaspoon fresh lemon juice
1   teaspoon onion juice
    Salt to taste
    Lemon slices for garnish

1. In a 3-quart casserole, combine the broccoli, cauliflower, and water, and cover. Cook on High 4 to 5 min-

utes, until brightly colored. Immediately rinse with cold water and drain.

2. Arrange the yellow pepper strips in the bottom of an 8-cup ring or Bundt pan. Place flowerets to the edges, stems together. Press and pack the vegetables and set them aside.

3. Combine the margarine, lemon juice, and onion juice in a 1-cup measure. Cook on Medium (50 percent) 30 to 60 seconds. Pour the mixture over the vegetables, and cover. Cook on High 4 to 6 minutes, or until hot.

4. Invert the pan onto serving platter and garnish the top with lemon slices.

For one serving:
Calories 81
Total fat, grams 2.3
Saturated fat, grams 0.4

Carbohydrate, grams 10
Protein, grams 5
Sodium, mg 17
Cholesterol, mg 0

BAKED SWEET POTATOES WITH ORANGE ZEST

SERVES 6

Sweet potatoes are as American as turkey, and a healthful complement to the Thanksgiving meal. Choose the moist, honey-flavored "Jewel" that many grocery stores label "yams." Other varieties are drier and less flavorful. While sweet potatoes can be grown as far north as New Jersey, they are a southern specialty. Many of the southern states grow delicious varieties that can only be found in the region—check your local farmers market for such varieties.

Baking is one of the most delicious and simplest ways to cook sweet potatoes. Baking brings out the

*natural sweetness, and who wants to mask that
flavor with a gummy syrup?*

*Sweet potatoes are power-packed with vitamin
A, vitamin B (especially thiamine), vitamin C, iron
and calcium, and some protein. Sweet potatoes are
a wonderful, easy food all through the year.*

**6   sweet potatoes, 6 to 8 ounces each
Zest of one orange**

1. Scrub and pierce the potatoes with a fork several times.
Place a paper towel on a trivet and put the sweet potatoes on top in spoke fashion. Cook on High for 18 to
21 minutes. Follow this simple chart for cooking times:

1 potato   — 4 to 5 minutes
2 potatoes— 6 to 7 minutes
4 potatoes—11 to 14 minutes
6 potatoes—18 to 21 minutes

2. Wrap the potatoes in paper towels and then in a terry-
cloth towel bundle. Let stand for 5 minutes or longer.

3. To serve, break open, peel, and garnish with orange
zest.

For one serving: Carbohydrate, grams 44
Calories 189   Protein, grams 3
Total fat, grams 0.2   Sodium, mg 19
Saturated fat, grams 0   Cholesterol, mg 0

THANKSGIVING GRAVY—TV

SERVES 6

¼   **cup all-purpose flour
Salt to taste**

⅛   teaspoon white pepper
2   cups low-fat turkey* or chicken stock, homemade
    (or broth, bouillon, or consommé)
    Dash liquid browning agent for color (optional)

1. Mix the flour, salt, and pepper together in a 6- to 8- cup measure. Add ¼ cup of the stock and whisk to make a smooth paste. Stir in the remaining stock slowly, whisking until smooth.

2. Cover and cook on High 5 to 8 minutes, or until thickened. Stir about every minute. Add the optional browning agent for color, if you wish.

TIP: The gravy will boil over quickly. Using a large container saves cleaning the microwave.

For one serving: Carbohydrate, grams 5
Calories 28   Protein, grams 1
Total fat, grams 0.4   Sodium, mg 8
Saturated fat, grams .09   Cholesterol, mg 0

CRANBERRY SAUCE

SERVES 6

2   tablespoons apple juice
1   tablespoon grated orange zest
1   cup of sugar
    Dash cinnamon
    Dash ground cloves

*As an alternative to chicken stock, you may make stock with the heart, liver, gizzard, and neck of the turkey, collectively called "giblets." They are usually packed in a small paper bag and stored in the cavity of the turkey. Simmer them conventionally in 3 to 4 cups of water for 1 to 1½ hours. Discard the fat from the stock and use the stock to prepare the gravy. Discard the giblets, as they are very high in cholesterol.

¼   teaspoon pure vanilla extract
1   12-ounce package fresh cranberries
      (about 3 cups)

1. Mix the juice, orange zest, sugar, cinnamon, cloves, vanilla extract, and cranberries together in a 4- to 6-cup measure.

2. Cook on High 6 to 8 minutes or until the skins of the berries just begin to "pop." Chill before serving.

For one serving: Carbohydrate, grams 35
Calories 140   Protein, grams 0
Total fat, grams 0   Sodium, mg 2
Saturated fat, grams 0   Cholesterol, mg 0

PUMPKIN-VANILLA PUDDING—TV

SERVES 6

Layer each pudding in a parfait glass and garnish with a dollop of vanilla yogurt and grated nutmeg. Start and end with the pumpkin pudding.

⅓   cup sugar
2   tablespoons cornstarch
1   tablespoon all-purpose flour
½   teaspoon apple-pie spice
1   cup canned or cooked pumpkin
1   cup skim milk
1   recipe of vanilla pudding (see below)
     Vanilla yogurt for garnish
     Grated nutmeg for garnish

1. In a 6- or 8-cup measure, stir together the sugar, cornstarch, flour, and spice. Set aside. In another, similar

container, combine the pumpkin and milk. Whisk the dry ingredients into the liquid ingredients, and cover.

2. Cook on High 6 to 12 minutes. Stir after the first 2 minutes, then after every minute until thickened and bubbly. Place a layer of wax paper directly on the pudding, then chill.

VANILLA PUDDING

- 1 tablespoon cornstarch
- 3 tablespoons sugar
- 1 cup skim milk
- 3 egg whites
- ½ teaspoon pure vanilla extract
- 2 drops yellow food coloring (optional)

1. Combine the cornstarch and sugar in a small bowl and mix thoroughly.

2. Combine the milk, egg whites, vanilla extract and food coloring in a 4- to 6-cup measure. Whisk to blend. Add the dry ingredients and whisk all the ingredients together thoroughly and cover.

3. Cook on High 3 to 4 minutes or until thick, stirring after every minute. To chill, place wax paper directly on the pudding and refrigerate.

For one serving:
Calories 131
Total fat, grams 0.3
Saturated fat, grams .06

Carbohydrate, grams 28
Protein, grams 5
Sodium, mg 69
Cholesterol, mg 1

Menu 20.

A Winter Meal

My Mom's Meat Loaf*

"Skinny" Mashed Potatoes*

Lemon Broccoli*

Apple Crumble*

MY MOM'S MEAT LOAF

SERVES 4

This is an adaption of my mother's meat loaf. No, my mother didn't use ground turkey, and she didn't use bran flakes, but she would have if she had known what havoc the fat was going to create for my brother.

Mom's Meat Loaf is soft and moist, rather than hard and dense. And yes, you can make it with all ground beef if you prefer—just be sure to choose lean ground round, rather than the fattier chuck or "ground meat." Purchase turkey breast and have it ground without the skin. Much of the prepackaged ground turkey is ground with the skin added, which raises the fat content considerably.

I like to make doubles of this recipe and put one loaf in the freezer. (The truth is that I make five pounds of meat loaf and divide the mixture into five loaves and freeze them!)

Meat loaf sandwiches are good too. Just ask Tex. . . .

½ green bell pepper, chopped
1 medium yellow onion, chopped
½ pound ground turkey
½ pound ground round
2 egg whites

2   ½ cups bran flakes
½   teaspoon black pepper
1   8-ounce can tomato sauce, no salt added
1½ tablespoons fresh thyme (or ½ teaspoon dried)

1. Combine the green pepper and onion in a 2-cup measure and cover. Cook on High 2 minutes. Drain and set aside.

2. In another 6- to 8-cup container, combine the ground meats, egg whites, bran flakes, black pepper, and three fourths of the tomato sauce. Add the onion-and-pepper mixture to the meat mixture, and blend. Place the mixture on a utility rack and shape into a loaf. Brush with the remaining tomato sauce. Cover with wax paper.

3. Cook on High 9 to 12 minutes. Let stand 5 minutes, covered with aluminum foil.

TIP: To increase complex carbohydrates and fiber in your diet and decrease fat, substitute ½ cup mashed cooked Great Northern beans for ½ pound of ground meat.

For one serving: Carbohydrate, grams 26
Calories 299   Protein, grams 24
Total fat, grams 11   Sodium, mg 317
Saturated fat, grams 3.8   Cholesterol, mg 56

"SKINNY" MASHED POTATOES

SERVES 4

1   pound medium russet potatoes, unpeeled
1   tablespoon water
1   teaspoon unsalted vegetable-oil margarine
1   leek

½ cup skim milk
Salt and pepper to taste

1. Scrub and cut each potato in 4 or 6 pieces. Place in a
   4- to 6-cup measure. Add the water and cover. Cook on
   High 6 to 7 minutes and let stand 5 minutes. Drain and
   discard most of the liquid.

2. Place the margarine in a 1-cup measure. To melt, cook
   on medium (50 percent) for 15 seconds. Set aside.

3. Cut the leek in half lengthwise, and wash it thoroughly
   to remove the sand. Cut it into ½-inch slices, using all
   of the white portion and up to 1 inch of the green stems.
   Add the leeks to the margarine and cover. Cook on High
   1 minute and add them to the potatoes. Mash them together with an electric mixer.

4. Put the milk in a 1-cup measure and cook on High for
   1 minute. Add to the mashed potatoes and blend thoroughly. Add salt and pepper to taste.

TIP: About 4 or 5 medium potatoes will make 1 pound.

For one serving: Carbohydrate, grams 32
Calories 155   Protein, grams 4
Total fat, grams 1.2   Sodium, mg 28
Saturated fat, grams 0.3 Cholesterol, mg 0

LEMON BROCCOLI

SERVES 4

*We have eaten broccoli prepared this way for years.
I can't imagine anyone improving on this simple
combination. Broccoli is such a healthy vegetable*

to have on hand to munch on, as part of a meal or stashed in the refrigerator, for those (many) odd moments when I want to devour "something" (even though I'd rather it be a cookie).

Broccoli is rich in vitamin A and C, both important nutrients that many people don't have enough of in their diets. I hope Lemon Broccoli becomes your favorite too.

> 1   bunch broccoli
> 1   teaspoon unsalted vegetable-oil margarine
> 1   teaspoon fresh lemon juice

1. Wash and remove the thick stems of the broccoli. Place the florets toward the center and stalks toward the edge of a 2-quart container, and cover. Cook on High 4 to five minutes, or until tender. Let stand 1 to 2 minutes.

2. Put margarine in a 1-cup measure. To melt, cook on Medium (50 percent) 15 to 30 seconds. Add the lemon juice to the melted margarine and pour over the broccoli.

For one serving:	Carbohydrate, grams 3
Calories 25	Protein, grams 1
Total fat, grams 1	Sodium, mg 5
Saturated fat, grams 0.2	Cholesterol, mg 0

APPLE CRUMBLE

SERVES 6

The Washington Apple Commission provided the inspiration for this yummy dessert. I made some changes to cut the calories so that you can enjoy this fall's harvest with a healthier heart. Use Golden

Delicious or other yellow-skinned baking apples that are native to your part of the country. Red-skinned baking apples will work well, but I think the dish is prettier with the golden beauties.

I have left the peels on the apples for the extra fiber and nutrients provided there, but you may prefer to remove them.

1½ pounds Golden Delicious apples (3 or 4), cored and sliced
2   tablespoons fresh lemon juice
¼   cup all-purpose flour
¼   cup packed brown sugar
½   teaspoon allspice
2   tablespoons unsalted vegetable-oil margarine
2   tablespoons chopped nuts (optional)
    Low-fat vanilla yogurt (optional)

1. Place the apples in an 8- or 9-inch flat round baking dish. Coat them with lemon juice to prevent darkening.

2. In a small mixing bowl, blend the flour, sugar, allspice, and margarine with a fork or pastry blender. Add the optional nuts and mix well.

3. Sprinkle the mixture over the apples and cook, uncovered, on High for 10 to 12 minutes. Let stand 5 minutes. Serve warm.

Tip: Tex pours a couple of tablespoons of low-fat vanilla yogurt over his Apple Crumble.

For one serving: Carbohydrate, grams 30
Calories 160   Protein, grams 1
Total fat, grams 4   Sodium, mg 3
Saturated fat, grams 0.8   Cholesterol, mg 0

Menu 21.

Valley-Girl Night

*Jackie's Saucy Fish**

*Savory Long-Grain and Wild Rice**

*Spicy Baked Tomatoes**

*Coco-Oat Brownies**

JACKIE'S SAUCY FISH

SERVES 4

What a great friend to have—one who "donates" a great recipe to someone else's cookbook! Long before that happened, I knew I would like this woman. She's from Virginia too (and you know about how I feel about Virginia). Of course, we had other areas of common interest.

Jackie Tulloh and I worked together for a number of years while I was in the retail microwave world. We taught classes together, laughed a lot, and spent many hours talking about growing up in small towns in Virginia. Our mothers were a favorite topic—on how they cooked, or didn't. I'd bring up a favorite recipe, and she would say, "Oh, that's Valley (Shenandoah Valley) food. I ate that when I was going to James Madison."

You see, even though Virginia is a small state, it has many food as well as cultural idiosyncrasies. This recipe is definitely not "Valley food," but everywhere food, and oh, so easy and so delicious. It's great "company food" too. Thanks, Jackie, and Valley girls everywhere.

1   pound orange roughy (or flounder or sole)
1   tablespoon olive oil
4   cloves garlic, minced

1   bunch green onions and tops, chopped
½   cup fresh mushrooms, sliced
⅓   cup green bell pepper, chopped
⅓   cup red bell pepper, chopped
¼   to ½ teaspoon cayenne pepper (go slowly if you don't like hot!)
1   tablespoon fresh lemon juice
     Salt to taste

1. Pat the fish fillets dry with a paper towel and place in a 12″ × 8″ × 2″ baking dish. Fold under the thin ends of the fish for even cooking. Set aside.

2. Place the oil, garlic, onions, mushrooms, both bell peppers, cayenne pepper, lemon juice, and salt in a 4- to 6-cup measure and cover. Cook on High 3 minutes and stir. Cook on High 2 to 3 minutes, or until heated throughout.

3. Spoon the sauce over the fish fillets. Cover with wax paper and cook on High 3 to 4 minutes, or until fish flakes easily with a fork. Let stand, covered, for 3 minutes.

For one serving: Carbohydrate, grams 2
Calories 76   Protein, grams 8
Total fat, grams 4   Sodium, mg 31
Saturated fat, grams 0.6   Cholesterol, mg 19

SAVORY LONG-GRAIN AND WILD RICE

MAKES 4

½   cup yellow onions, chopped
¾   cup celery without leaves, chopped
1   teaspoon olive oil

  1 6-ounce package long-grain and wild rice (discard
       seasoning packet*)
 2½ cups low-fat chicken stock, homemade (or broth,
       bouillon, or consommé)
  1 tablespoon fresh tarragon (or 1 teaspoon dried)
     Salt to taste
     Fresh chopped parsley for garnish

1. Put the onions, celery, and oil in a 2- to 2½-quart dish
   and cover. Cook on High 3 to 4 minutes or until the
   vegetables are soft. Discard the liquid.

2. Add the rice mixture (without seasoning packet), stock,
   marjoram, and (optional) salt to the onion/celery mixture, and cover. Cook on High 6 to 7 minutes and then
   cook on Medium (50 percent) for 20 minutes. Let stand,
   covered, 5 minutes. Fluff with a fork and serve. Garnish with chopped parsley, if desired.

TIP: If you serve this rice dish with a different entrée, you
might wish to substitute the chopped yellow onions with
chopped green onions with tops. Set aside some of the
green tops as a garnish.

For one serving: Carbohydrate, grams 14
Calories 85   Protein, grams 3
Total fat, grams 1.9   Sodium, mg 34
Saturated fat, grams 0.3   Cholesterol, mg 0

SPICY BAKED TOMATOES

SERVES 4

  4 large tomatoes, cored and halved crosswise
  1 tablespoon spicy brown mustard

*The seasoning packet that comes with the rice is very high in sodium.

1   teaspoon olive oil
¼   cup green onions, white and part of tops, chopped
1   tablespoon fresh basil, chopped (or 1 teaspoon dried)
     Parsley sprigs or basil for garnish (optional)

1. Put the tomatoes in a 12″×8″×2″ flat baking dish. Spread the mustard on each half.

2. In a 1-cup measure, mix together the oil, onion, and basil. cook on High 1 minute, or until the onions are soft. Spoon the onion mixture over each tomato, and cover.

3. Cook on High 3 to 5 minutes. Garnish with parsley or basil.

For one serving: Carbohydrate, grams 8
Calories 53   Protein, grams 2
Total fat, grams 1.4   Sodium, mg 13
Saturated fat, grams 0.2   Cholesterol, mg 0

COCO-OAT BROWNIES

MAKES 16

⅓   cup unsalted vegetable oil margarine
⅓   cup white sugar
¼   cup packed brown sugar
1½ teaspoons pure vanilla extract
1   whole egg, slightly beaten
2   egg whites, slightly beaten
¼   cup cocoa
½   teaspoon baking powder
⅔   cups cake flour
3   tablespoons quick-cooking oatmeal
3   tablespoons chopped nuts (optional)

1. Place the margarine in a 4- to 6-cup measure. To melt, cook on medium (50 percent) for 2½ to 4 minutes. Add the 2 sugars and vanilla extract and mix well. Stir in the eggs.

2. In a separate container, sift together the cocoa, baking powder, and flour. Add the dry ingredients to the sugar/egg mixture and mix 1 minute on Medium speed of an electric mixer. Stir in the oatmeal and optional nuts.

3. Spoon evenly into the prepared pan and shield the corners with about 1 inch of foil. (Don't let the foil touch the sides of the microwave.) Cook on High 1 minute and remove the foil. Cook on High another 2 to 4 minutes, being careful not to overcook. Let stand covered with wax paper for 5 minutes. "Dust" with powdered sugar if desired.

For one serving:
Calories 88
Total fat, grams 4
Saturated fat, grams 0.8

Carbohydrate, grams 11
Protein, grams 2
Sodium, mg 21
Cholesterol, mg 17

CHAPTER 11

Kitchen Basics

ഇഇഇ

    These basics will help you prepare many of the recipes in the book. The chicken stock, for example, is used extensively to add flavor with less sodium and fat than commercial stocks or broths. The poached chicken itself is a staple that goes into many recipes.

Others, like the Easy Italian Sauce, were just so basic and so important that I couldn't bear to leave them out. You will find the sauce useful for those nights when you want a quick dinner—it goes well over chicken or pasta or fish.

Easy Italian Sauce*

Heavenly Low-Fat Cheese Sauce*

Nonfat Yogurt Cheese*

Poached Chicken and Stock*

"Un"traditional Hollandaise Sauce*

EASY ITALIAN SAUCE

SERVES 4

This sauce is so easy and tasty, you could serve it over ice cream—if you still ate ice cream. Try the sauce over pasta, chicken, or fish instead. If you do have leftovers, find room in your freezer for them!

2 teaspoons olive oil
1 medium yellow onion, chopped
2 15-ounce cans Italian stewed tomatoes, drained
2 tablespoons fresh basil, chopped (or 1 tablespoon dried)

1. Combine the oil and onions in a 2-quart casserole and cover. Cook on High 3 to 4 minutes, or until onions are soft.

2. Mash the tomatoes with a potato masher or crush thoroughly with a spoon. Add the tomatoes and basil to the onions, stir, and cover. Cook on High 5 minutes. Cook, uncovered, on Mediium-High (70 percent) 10 to 15 minutes or Medium (50 percent) 20 to 45 minutes to blend flavors and reduce liquid.

TIP: For a smoother sauce, pulse in the food processor.

For one serving: Carbohydrate, grams 15
Calories 89   Protein, grams 2
Total fat, grams 2.4   Sodium, mg 425
Saturated fat, grams 0.3 Cholesterol, mg 0

HEAVENLY LOW-FAT CHEESE SAUCE

SERVES 8

> *This recipe uses a cheddar-flavored low-fat cheese. Several companies make these cheeses, and they can be found in most grocery stores. Look for the brand with the lowest amount of fat.*

> 2 tablespoons unsalted vegetable-oil margarine
> 2 tablespoons all-purpose flour
> 1 cup skim milk
> ¼ cup nonfat yogurt (or low-fat)
> Salt to taste
> 1 cup shredded low-fat cheddar cheese
> ¼ teaspoon turmeric
> Dash white pepper

1. Put margarine in a 2-cup measure. To melt, cook on Medium (50 percent) for 1 to 1½ minues. Add the flour and whisk to make a paste. Stir in the milk. Cover and cook on High for 3 to 3½ minutes, stirring after every minute, until thickened.

2. Add the yogurt and salt and stir. Add the cheese, turmeric, and pepper gradually and stir to blend. If the cheese is not thoroughly blended, cook on Medium (50 percent) for 30 seconds to melt. Be careful not to overcook—cheese quickly becomes tough and stringy.

For one serving: Carbohydrate, grams 4
Calories 104   Protein, grams 8
Total fat, grams 8   Sodium, mg 8
Saturated fat, grams 0.6   Cholesterol, mg 1

NONFAT YOGURT CHEESE

MAKES 2 cups

Use yogurt cheese for making low-fat cheesecake, dips, as a spread for toast, or served with fruit sauce as a light dessert. As no "official" nutritive values for yogurt cheese are available, the ones listed are estimates.

1   32-ounce container of nonfat yogurt, without gelatin

1. Line a strainer with cheesecloth or 2 coffeepot filters. Set over a deep bowl, and spoon the yogurt into the strainer. Cover and refrigerate overnight.

2. The next day, discard or use the accumulated liquid* from the bowl and spoon the yogurt cheese into a storage container and refrigerate. The yogurt cheese will stay fresh several weeks.

Tip: For an alternative method for making yogurt cheese, you can order the Really Creamy Yogurt Cheese Funnel for about $12 to $14 (see Appendix E).

For 2 cups: Carbohydrate, grams 34
Calories 284   Protein, grams 36
Total fat, grams 0.5   Sodium, mg 320
Saturated fat, grams 0   Cholesterol, mg 1.6

*The accumulated liquid is the whey. It is high in protein and very nutritious. Use it for part of the liquid in breads and muffins.

POACHED CHICKEN AND STOCK

SERVES 5

1 2½- to 3-pound whole fryer (use all the parts but the liver, gizzard, and heart)
2 cups low-fat chicken stock, homemade (or broth, bouillon, or consommé)
2 cups room-temperature water
12 stalks celery without leaves, cut to fit the container
½ medium leek
1 cup fresh parsley, stalks and leaves
4 black or white peppercorns (or ½ teaspoon ground pepper)
   Salt to taste

1. Under cold running water, thoroughly wash the chicken inside and out.

2. Put the chicken breast-side down in a 4-quart container. Add enough stock and water to come halfway up the chicken. Cover and cook on High for 15 minutes. Uncover and remove any residue that has accumulated.

3. Turn the chicken over, and add the remaining liquid (if available), celery, leek, parsley, peppercorns, and salt, and cover. Cook on High for 7 to 10 minutes, or until chicken near the bone is no longer pink. When the chicken is cool enough to handle, discard the bones and skin. Strain the stock. Use the stock and chicken immediately or freeze them separately.

TIP: To defat the stock, refrigerate it overnight. The next day, skim the fat from the top while it is very cold.

For one serving:
Calories 389
Total fat, grams 13
Saturated fat, grams 3.6

Carbohydrate, grams 5
Protein, grams 63
Sodium, mg 207
Cholesterol, mg 179

"UN"TRADITIONAL HOLLANDAISE SAUCE

SERVES 8

¼ cup unsalted vegetable-oil margarine
½ cup egg substitute (or 4 egg whites)*
½ teaspoon dry mustard
2 tablespoons fresh lemon juice
Salt to taste
Dash cayenne

1. Put the margarine in a 2-cup measure and cook on Medium (50 percent) 2½ to 3½ minutes.

2. Add the eggs, dry mustard, lemon juice, and seasonings, whisk thoroughly, and cover. Cook on Medium (50 percent) for 2 minutes, whisking thoroughly every 30 seconds until light and thickened.

TIP: The sauce is done when it falls off the whisk in thick drops.

For one serving:
Calories 76
Total fat, grams 7
Saturated fat, grams 1.4

Carbohydrate, grams 1
Protein, grams 2
Sodium, mg 30
Cholesterol, mg 0

*If using egg whites, add a dash or 2 of yellow food coloring to add color. Otherwise the sauce will be very pale.

APPENDIX A

How to Determine Wattage

✿✿✿

The following test should give you a *rough* idea of the approximate wattage of your microwave. Of course, wattage output depends on the power coming into your house (input). Expect your results to be 10 or more percent below the manufacturer's specifications. I had a burning desire to learn output wattage on my microwaves. The test and my results follow:

1. Fill a 2-cup glass measure with distilled water. Bring the water to 65 degrees F* (use ice cubes to cool the water if necessary), stirring with a cooking thermometer.

2. Cook on High 1 minute. Stir 5 times clockwise and 5 times counterclockwise with the thermometer (I know this sounds weird, but you want to equalize the tem-

---

*One degree F difference in water temperature changes the wattage output reading by as much as seventy watts!

perature), and check the temperature immediately. The temperature was 97 F.

3. Subtract 65 from 97 = 32 degrees F difference.

4. Multiply 32 × 17.5 (a standard)* 4 = 562 is the approximate wattage output of my "600 watt" microwave.

NOTE: During the test, the air-conditioning was running in my fifty-year-old house. Normal daytime kitchen lights were on.

Of course I *do not* present this exercise as any scientific experiment, but as a point of interest. You can see how many variables affect the wattage output reading: the temperature of the water, the temperature of the room, the water-stirring method, how quickly you remove the water from the microwave and check the temperature, even the type of water you use. These variables explain better why microwave recipes give a range of cooking times in the instructions. See page 113.

*One company uses 18.5 as a standard. No reason is given. By using 18.5, the wattage of the same microwave would be 592 watts! Excuse me, I have headache number 8.

APPENDIX B

Addresses for More Information

శ్రశ్రశ్ర

American Dietetic Association
216 West Jackson Boulevard
Chicago, Illinois 60606-6995
312-899-0040

American Heart Association
National Center
7320 Greenville Avenue
Dallas, Texas 47231
214-706-1364

U.S. Department of Agriculture Meat and Poultry
Hot line: 1-800-535-4555

APPENDIX C

Equivalents and Substitutions

❧❧❧

How many drops in a dash or dribbles in a splash?
Or how much juice in a lemon or tablespoons in a cup? I
hope this chart will help. Use the chart with the *Save Your
Heart with Susan* recipes.

EQUIVALENTS

Measurements:

A dash   2 to 3 drops or less than ⅛ teaspoon
A splash
A pinch

1 tablespoon	3 teaspoons
¼ cup	4 tablespoons
½ cup	8 tablespoons
1 cup	16 tablespoons
1 pint	2 cups
1 quart	4 cups
1 gallon	4 quarts

Foods:

Apples, 1 pound	3 medium
Apples, 1 pound	3 cups diced
Bananas, 1 pound	3 medium
Berries, 1 pint	1¾ cups
Cheese, ¼ pound	1 cup shredded
Cheese, creamed, 3 oz.	6 tablespoons
Chicken, 1 broiler	4 servings
Chicken, 1 broiler	2½ to 3 cups cooked meat
Chicken breast halves, 2	1 pound
Egg whites, ½ cup	4 to 5 whites
Lemon, 1 medium	2–3 tablespoons juice and about 1 tablespoon grated peel
Potatoes, 1 pound	3 medium (2¼ cup diced)
Tomatoes, 1 pound	3 medium

SUBSTITUTIONS

When the recipe says:	*Use these Save Your Heart substitutions:*
1 cup butter, shortening, or lard	1 cup margarine or ¾ cup oil
1 cup whole milk	1 cup skim milk
1 cup light cream	1 cup evaporated skim milk
1 cup sour cream	1 cup plain nonfat yogurt
1 whole egg	2 egg whites or ¼ cup egg substitute or 1 egg white + 1 teaspoon oil
1 ounce (a square) chocolate	3 tablespoons cocoa + 1 tablespoon vegetable oil
Ground meat	Ground turkey, ground round

APPENDIX D

Internal Temperatures
of Cooked Foods

ಜಜಜ

Food Temperatures

Foods cook quickly in the microwave. Using a thermometer or temperature probe to measure the internal temperature can prevent "rock formations" in your prize roast or Thanksgiving turkey. Respect the minimum cooking temperatures for the safety of your food. Some guidelines follow:

Beef:
    Rare: 140 degrees
    Medium: 160 degrees
    Well Done: 170 degrees
    Ground Beef: 150–170 degrees
Pork:
    Ham, Smoked: 160 degrees
    Ham, Fresh: 160 degrees
    Roasts: 160–170 degrees
Lamb Roasts:
    Rare: 140 degrees

Medium: 160 degrees
Well Done: 170–175 degrees
Veal: 170 degrees
Poultry:
   Boneless Turkey Roast: 170–175 degrees
   Turkey w/Bone: 185 degrees
   Other Poultry: 180–185 degrees
   Center of Stuffing: 165 degrees
Game:
  Venison (Deer):   160–170 degrees
  Rabbit: 180–185 degrees

Previously cooked food that is warmed after being frozen should be at least 140 degrees F in several places.

Manufacturers and Suppliers

ଊଊଊ

Company	Item	Telephone
Eagle Affiliates	Cookware	800-221-0988
Micro-Trim	Trim Kits	800-338-8746 in CA: 800-241-7046
MicroCare	Microwave Cleaner	800-289-9927
Polyvinyl Film	Plastic Wrap	800-343-6134
Rubbermaid	Cookware	216-264-6464 (collect)
Tara Products	Cookware	800-343-6060
Triad Communications	Yogurt Cheese Funnel	800-525-6902

MICROWAVE OVEN REPAIR

To obtain service for your microwave, call the numbers below for referral to the closest repair service in your area. All of these numbers are subject to change, of course. When all else fails, look on your Owner's Manual or in the telephone book.

1. Amana	(800) 843-0304
2. Avanti	(800) 323-5029
3. Brother	(800) 981-0300
4. Frigidaire	(800) 451-7007
5. Goldstar	(800) 255-2550
6. GE/Hotpoint	(800) 626-2000
7. Hitachi	(800) 447-2882
8. Kitchen Aid	(800) 422-1230
9. Magic Chef	(800) 255-2370
10. Panasonic	(800) 447-4700
11. Quasar	(800) 447-4700
12. Samsung	(800) 447-2882
13. Sanyo	(201) 641-2333
14. Sharp	(800) 526-0264
15. Sunbeam	(800) 323-7303
16. Tappan	(800) 245-0600
17. Thermador	(800) 526-1133
18. Toshiba	(800) 221-0314
19. White/Westinghouse	(800) 245-0600
20. Whirlpool	(800) 253-1301

Below is an "all else" address. When all else fails you may send your problems to:

Major Appliance Consumer Action Panel
20 North Wacker Drive
Chicago, Illinois 60606

If you are writing to this group, they will need the following information: your name, address, daytime telephone, the type of appliance, brand, model, and serial number; the purchase date and price; the name, address, and telephone number of the local dealer or repair service; copies of all correspondence regarding your problem; copies of all service receipts; and a short and clear description of what you think is a reasonable solution to your problem.

And another reminder, when making a purchase, be sure you understand the conditions of the warranty and the location at which your microwave can be serviced if necessary.

APPENDIX F

Microwave Specialty Stores

୧୨୨୨

(Friedmans Microwave Ovens)

Alabama	Mobile (205) 343-3800
Arizona	Tuscon (602) 745-9876
California	Capitola (408) 462-4611
	Costa Mesa (714) 545-6080
	Cupertino (408) 996-9283
	Dublin (415) 829-2626
	Encino (818) 501-0794
	Eureka (707) 445-4999
	Fairfield (707) 426-0307
	Fresno (209) 224-0826
	Goleta (Santa Barbara) (805) 683-1596
	Hayward (415) 886-0575
	Long Beach (213) 598-7756
	Modesto (209) 522-1199
	Montclair (714) 625-2361
	Newark (415) 794-8838
	Oakland (415) 444-1119

Oakland Corporate Office: (415) 444-1139
Oceanside (619) 439-6440
Orange (714) 633-8000
Palo Alto (415) 324-1262
Pasadena (818) 577-2223
Pleasant Hill (415) 825-7877
Richmond (415) 222-5441
Sacramento (916) 966-3919
San Diego (619) 292-5444
San Francisco (415) 221-0888
(415) 431-5550
San José (408) 243-4600
San Luis Obispo (805) 544-9639
San Mateo (415) 347-6612
San Rafael (415) 479-9080*
Santa Maria (805) 928-4439
Santa Rosa (707) 523-2911
Stockton (209) 478-7217
Thousand Oaks (805) 496-3821
Ventura (805) 650-9838
Visalia (209) 627-2696

Illinois	Chicago (312) 248-4949
Iowa	Des Moines (515) 270-1234
Michigan	Grand Rapids (616) 956-9595
Nebraska	Lincoln (402) 483-2218
North Carolina	Durham (919) 688-4371
Oregon	Beaverton (503) 646-2288
	Eugene (503) 485-4200
	Medford (503) 772-9979
	Salem (503) 364-0538
Tennessee	Knoxville (615) 693-4344
Washington	Wenatchee (509) 663-5516

*Wendy and Susan's store.

APPENDIX G

Vegetable Cooking Guide

೫೫೫

(Refer to Chapter 9, page 127, for specific instructions)

FRESH VEGETABLES

Vegetable	Cooking Time for 1 lb on High Power†
Asparagus*	3½ to 5½ minutes
Broccoli Florets*	
Cauliflowerets	
Eggplant	
Leeks	
Mushrooms	
Onions, sliced, chopped	
Peas, English	

*See index for specific instructions
†Age, shape, size of vegetables, wattage of your microwave, and your own taste preferences are the best indicators for cooking times. The important word to emphasize in this chart is *guide*.

Spinach
Summer Squash (yellow, zuc-
   chini)*
Tomatoes, whole*

Broccoli Spears   5½ to 7½ minutes
Brussels Sprouts
Cabbage
Carrots*
Cauliflower, head
Corn-on-the-Cob*
Eggplant
Kohlrabi
Okra
Onions, whole
Peppers, whole (green, red)

Artichokes*   5 to 10 minutes
Beans, Green,* Wax
Baked Potatoes*
Beets (14–16 minutes/lb)
Greens*
Jicama
New Potatoes
Red Potatoes*
Parsnips
Pea Pods
Rutabagas
Sweet Potatoes*
Turnips
Winter Squash

1. Wash and place the vegetables in a casserole. Spritz or
   add 1 to 2 tablespoons of water. Use more water for
   older, drier, fibrous (green beans, broccoli), or larger
   quantities of vegetables. Additional water and cooking
   time will make vegetables softer. Pierce vegetables with
   skins (potatoes, acorn squash).

2. Cook covered on High power according to the times
   on the chart. Stir the vegetables and rearrange as nec-

essary. Let stand, covered, 2 to 5 minutes depending on the quantity.

3. Practice, practice, practice.

FROZEN VEGETABLES

1. Remove vegetables from box or bag (not pouch-type) and place them in a cooking container and cover. Cook on High 4 to 6 minutes (10 ounces) or 6 to 8 minutes (16 ounces).

2. For vegetables in a cooking pouch, slit the pouch twice and place it on a pie plate.

3. Frozen vegetables do not need to be defrosted before cooking.

4. Stir vegetables after half of the cooking time.

5. Let vegetables stand, covered, for 2 to 4 minutes after cooking.

Bibliography

Becker, Marion Rombauer, and Irma Rombauer. *The Joy of Cooking*. Indianapolis: Bobbs-Merrill, 1974.

Brody, Jane. *Jane Brody's Nutrition Book*. New York: W. W. Norton, 1981.

DeBakey, Michael, Gotto, Antonio, Scott, Lynne, and John Foreyt, *The Living Heart Diet*. New York: Fireside Books, 1986.

Fletcher, Anne M. *Eat Fish, Live Better*. New York: Harper & Row, 1989.

Franz, Marion, Betsy Hedding, and Gayle Leitch. *Opening the Door to Good Nutrition*. Minneapolis: International Diabetes Center, 1985.

Goor, Dr. Ron, and Nancy Goor. *Eater's Choice*. Boston: Houghton Mifflin, 1989.

Hillman, Howard. *Kitchen Science*. Boston: Houghton Mifflin, 1981.

Jester, Pat. *HP Books Microwave Cookbook—The Complete Guide*. Tucson, Ariz.: Fisher Publishing, 1983.

Lindsey, Anne. *American Cancer Society Cookbook*. New York: Hearst Books, 1988.

Methven, Barbara. *Basic Microwaving*. Minnetonka, Minn.: Cy DeCosse, Inc., 1988.

Methven, Barbara. *Microwave Cooking Fruits and Vegetables.* Minnetonka, Minn.: Cy DeCosse, Inc., 1981.

Methven, Barbara. *Microwaving Poultry and Seafood.* Minnetonka, Minn.: Cy DeCosse, Inc., 1986.

Microwave Guide and Cookbook. General Electric Company, 1983.

National Livestock and Meat Board. *Recommended Internal Temperatures for Meat Doneness.* Chicago: 1989.

National Research Council. *Recommended Dietary Allowances.* Washington, D.C.: National Academy Press, 1989.

"1990 Heart and Stroke Facts." Dallas: American Heart Association, 1989.

Pennington, Jean A. T. *Food Values of Portions Commonly Used,* 15th edition. New York: Harper & Row, 1989.

The Surgeon General's Report on Nutrition and Health. Washington, D.C.: U.S. Government Printing Office, 1988.

Van Zante, Helen J. *The Microwave Oven.* Boston: Houghton Mifflin, 1973.

Index

❧❧❧